DEBBIE MUMM'S® BIRDHOUSES
for every Season

These bright and beautiful birdhouse projects will fill your home
and garden with joy every season of the year.

DEBBIE MUMM®

DEAR FRIENDS,

I've always loved birdhouses! They have so much personality and charm ... they remind me of charming miniature versions of "people houses!" As you know from my fabric and other designs, I have fun painting them in all shapes and styles ... each with its own whimsical decorating touches!

In fact, I'm so fond of these delightful little domiciles that we've dedicated this entire book to bringing you birdhouse creations to cheerfully welcome each changing season. What a fun and fanciful touch to add to your home. Your family is sure to love them too!

So, for a charming new approach to decorating for the changing seasons ... think birdhouses! You can add a little whimsy to your kitchen table, guest bedroom, entryway, or any special spot that needs a cheerful touch. In fact, we've created a birdhouse wall quilt with a different theme for each of the four seasons. You'll have fun changing your décor as the weather changes outside your window!

Beautiful butterflies and blossoms join our garden gathering of birdhouse projects, and you'll find fresh, new ideas in each seasonal chapter. Simple-to-do painting ideas and a wonderful mosaic garden stone join the many quilting projects waiting for you to enjoy in Birdhouses for Every Season.

Whimsical and wonderful artwork adds a touch of magic to each chapter. I know it will make browsing through your book even more delightful as you turn each page to discover the charming art illustrating each season.

Relax and take a few minutes out of your busy day to sit back and enjoy your book. I hope it will bring a smile to your face and beautiful projects to your home.

Sincerely,

Debbie Mumm

TABLE OF CONTENTS

4 SPRING

6 *Trellis in Bloom Bed Quilt*
10 *Birdhouse Pillow Covers*
13 *Small Pillow Covers*
14 *Beautiful Butterflies Wall Quilt*
21 *Beautiful Butterflies Twin-Size Quilt*
22 *Butterfly House*
24 *Blossoms and Butterflies Table Quilt*

26 SUMMER

28 *Birdhouse Sampler Quilt*
43 *Sunset Birdhouse Table Runner*
44 *Garden Chapel Wallhanging*
50 *Lots of Ladybugs Quilt*
55 *Little Ladybug Wallhanging*
56 *Ladybug House*
58 *Garden Stepping Stone*
60 *Garden Tool Caddy*

62 AUTUMN

64 *Fall Flight Quilt*
68 *Back-To-School Birdhouse*
74 *Apple Harvest*
77 *Class Act*
78 *Falling Leaves Table Runner*
83 *Falling Leaves Placemats*

84 WINTER

86 *Birdhouse Border Christmas Quilt*
92 *Crimson Cardinals Table Quilt*
97 *Birdfeeder*
98 *Winter Birds Mantel Cover*
102 *Birdhouse Banner*

Spring

Beautiful birds and butterflies ... every year they announce that wonderfully welcome spring has finally arrived!

Soon our favorite feathered friends will settle into their backyard birdhouse homes and fluttering butterflies will join in the springtime welcome with their flights of fancy in and out of the fragrant blossoms.

This delightful vision of spring doesn't have to stay just in the garden. Bring the birdhouse whimsy indoors, too, with blooming-fresh projects created in the soft-as-a-breeze shades of spring.

Trellis in Bloom Bed Quilt

Bring the fresh colors and ordered elegance of a traditional English garden indoors as you spread this blooming creation atop a waiting bed.

Simple to piece, this generously-sized quilt is created with a single repeating block! Read all instructions before beginning and use ¼"-wide seam allowances throughout.

Trellis in Bloom Quilt
Finished Size: 93" x 105"
Photo: page 8

FABRIC REQUIREMENTS

Fabric A - 2¾ yards
Fabric B - 4¼ yards
Fabric C - 2¾ yards
Accent Border - ⅓ yard
Border - 1¼ yards *
Binding - ⅞ yard
Backing - 8⅛ yards
Lightweight Batting - 101" x 113"

* If you select a border print as we did, you will need to increase the yardage, depending on the number of design repeats in the fabric.

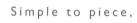

CUTTING THE STRIPS AND PIECES

Pre-wash and press fabrics. Using rotary cutter, see-through ruler, and cutting mat, cut the following strips and pieces. If indicated, some will need to be cut again into smaller strips and pieces. The approximate width of the fabric is 42". Measurements for all pieces include ¼"-wide seam allowance. Press in the direction of arrows.

		Number of Strips	Dimensions
	FABRIC A	4	4½" x 42"
		19	2½" x 42"
		4	6½" x 42"
	FABRIC B	22	2½" x 42"
		8	6½" x 42"
		7	4½" x 42"
	FABRIC C	4	4½" x 42"
		19	2½" x 42"
		4	6½" x 42"
	ACCENT BORDER	10	1" x 42"
	BORDER	10	4" x 42"
	BINDING	10	2¾" x 42"

MAKING THE BLOCKS

You will be making 56 lattice blocks. See Assembly Line Method on page 110, and use whenever possible.

1. Sew one 6½" x 42" Fabric B strip between one 2½" x 42" Fabric A strip and one 4½" x 42" Fabric A strip to make four 12½" x 42" strip sets as shown. Press. Using rotary cutter and ruler, cut fifty-six 2½" segments from strip sets. Label them unit 1.

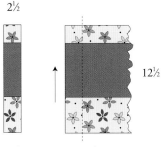

2½

12½

unit 1
Make 4 strip sets
Cut 56

2. Sew one 2½" x 42" Fabric B strip, one 6½" x 42" Fabric C strip, one 2½" x 42" Fabric A strip, and one 2½" x 42" Fabric C strip in order shown to make four 12½" x 42" strip sets. Press. Using rotary cutter and ruler, cut fifty-six 2½" segments from strip sets. Label them unit 2.

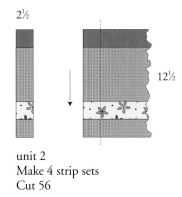

2½

12½

unit 2
Make 4 strip sets
Cut 56

3. Sew one 2½" x 42" Fabric B strip, one 2½" x 42" Fabric C strip, one 4½" x 42" Fabric B strip, one 2½" x 42" Fabric A strip, and one 2½" x 42" Fabric B strip in order shown to make seven 12½" x 42" strip sets. Press. Using rotary cutter and ruler, cut fifty-six 4½" segments from strip sets. Label them unit 3.

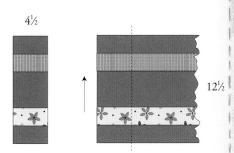

4½

12½

unit 3
Make 7 strip sets
Cut 56

4. Sew one 2½" x 42" Fabric A strip, one 2½" x 42" Fabric C strip, one 6½" x 42" Fabric A strip, and one 2½" x 42" Fabric B strip in order shown to make four 12½" x 42" strip sets. Press. Using rotary cutter and ruler, cut fifty-six 2½" segments from strip sets. Label them unit 4.

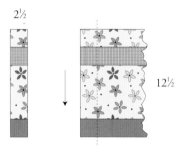

unit 4
Make 4 strip sets
Cut 56

5. Sew one 4½" x 42" Fabric C strip, one 6½" x 42" Fabric B strip, and one 2½" x 42" Fabric C strip in order shown to make four 12½" x 42" strip sets. Press. Using rotary cutter and ruler, cut fifty-six 2½" segments from strip sets. Label them unit 5.

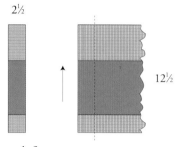

unit 5
Make 4 strip sets
Cut 56

6. Arrange and sew units 1 through 5 as shown. Make 56 blocks. Press 28 blocks toward unit 5 and 28 blocks toward unit 1. Block will measure 12½" square.

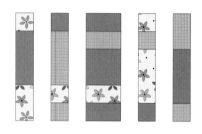

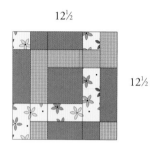

Make 56

ASSEMBLY

1. Refer to layout on page 6 and color photo. Arrange blocks in eight horizontal rows of seven blocks each. Sew blocks into rows. Press seams in opposite directions from row to row.

2. Sew rows together. Press.

3. Sew 1" x 42" accent border strips end to end to make one continuous 1" strip. Measure quilt from side to side through center. Cut two 1"-wide accent border strips to that measurement. Sew to top and bottom. Press seams toward border strips.

4. Measure quilt through center from top to bottom, including borders just added. Cut two 1"-wide border strips to that measurement. Sew to sides. Press.

5. Sew 4" x 42" border strips end to end to make one continuous 4"-wide strip. Measure quilt through center from side to side. Cut two 4"-wide border strips to that measurement. Sew to top and bottom. Press seams toward border strips.

6. Measure quilt through center from top to bottom, including borders just added. Cut two 4"-wide border strips to that measurement. Sew to sides. Press.

LAYERING AND FINISHING

1. Cut backing fabric crosswise into three equal pieces. Sew pieces together to make one 98" x 120" (approximate) backing piece. Arrange and baste backing, batting, and top together, referring to Layering the Quilt directions on page 111.

2. Machine or hand quilt as desired.

3. Sew eight 2¾" x 42" binding strips together in pairs. Cut two remaining strips in half and sew halves to each pieced strip. Refer to Binding the Quilt directions on page 111 to finish.

Birdhouse Pillow Covers

Birdhouse Pillow Covers
Finished Size: 34" x 24"
Photo: page 12

You'll love this *perky pillow cover with its morning-fresh colors and crisp flanged edges. It pairs up perfectly with our lovely Trellis in Bloom Bed Quilt, but you can display it anyplace you want to spread a touch of spring.*

Instructions here are *for a single sham, but they're so quick and easy you'll want to make more than one! Read all instructions before beginning, and use ¼"-wide seams throughout.*

FABRIC REQUIREMENTS

Fabric A (Background) - ¼ yard
Fabric B (Upper House) - ¼ yard
Fabric C (Middle House) - ⅛ yard
Fabric D (Lower House) - ¼ yard
Fabric E (Grass) - ⅛ yard
Roof Appliqués - ⅛ yard
Birdhouse Hole Appliqué - Scrap

Accent Border - ⅛ yard
Second Border - ⅛ yard
Third Border - ⅓ yard
Outside Border - ⅜ yard
Back Panels - 1⅜ yards
Lining - ⅞ yard
Lightweight Batting - 38" x 28" piece

CUTTING THE STRIPS AND PIECES

Read first paragraph of Cutting the Strips and Pieces on page 7.

	FIRST CUT		SECOND CUT	
	Number of Strips or Pieces	Dimensions	Number of Pieces	Dimensions
FABRIC A	2 2 2	6½" squares 2½" x 6½" 3½" x 9½"		
FABRIC B	1	12½" x 6½"		
FABRIC C	1	10½" x 2½"		
FABRIC D	1	10½" x 7½"		
FABRIC E	1	1½" x 16½"		
ROOF APPLIQUÉ	2	1¼" x 9½"		
ACCENT BORDER	2	1½" x 42"	2 2	1½" x 16½" 1½" x 18½"
SECOND BORDER	1	1½" x 42"	2	1½" x 18½"
THIRD BORDER	3	3½" x 42"	2 2	3½" x 20½" 3½" x 24½"
OUTSIDE BORDER	2	4½" x 42"	2	4½" x 24½"
BACK PANELS	2	24½" x 22½"		
LINING	1	38" x 28" piece		

BLOCK ASSEMBLY

You'll be making one birdhouse block. Whenever possible, use the Assembly Line Method on page 110.

1. Refer to Quick Corner Triangle directions on page 110. Sew two 6½" Fabric A squares to 12½" x 6½" Fabric B piece as shown. Press.

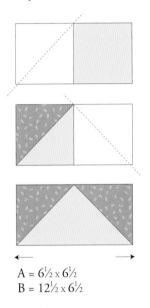

A = 6½ x 6½
B = 12½ x 6½

2. Sew unit from step 1 between two 2½" x 6½" Fabric A pieces. Press.

2½   2½

6½

3. Sew 10½" x 2½" Fabric C piece to 10½" x 7½" Fabric D piece as shown. Press.

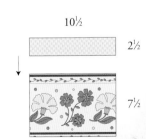

10½

2½

7½

APPLIQUÉ

1. Trace appliqué design from page 37. Make template and use scrap to cut one of birdhouse hole #2. Cut out appliqué, adding ¼" seam allowance.

2. Machine stitch or refer to Hand Appliqué directions on page 110. Appliqué two 1¼" x 9½" roof strips over roof. Follow seam lines, and square ends as shown. Refer to layout on page 10 and appliqué birdhouse hole to middle house strip.

PILLOW COVER ASSEMBLY

1. Layer batting between top and lining. Baste. Hand or machine quilt as desired. Trim batting and lining even with raw edge of sham top.

2. Machine stitch ¼"-wide hem along one 24½" edge of each 24½" x 22½" back panel. Fold hemmed edges 3" to wrong side and pin.

4. Sew unit from step 3 between two 3½" x 9½" Fabric A pieces. Press.

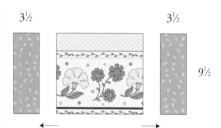

3½   3½

9½

5. Refer to layout on page 10. Arrange and sew unit from step 2, unit from step 4, and 1½" x 16½" Fabric E strip in order shown to make a vertical row.

BORDERS

1. Sew 1½" x 16½" accent border strips to top and bottom of block. Press seams toward borders. Sew 1½" x 18½" accent border strips to sides. Press.

2. Sew 1½" x 18½" second border strips to sides. Press seams away from center block.

3. Sew 3½" x 20½" third border strips to top and bottom. Press away from center block. Sew 3½" x 24½" third border strips to sides. Press.

4. Sew 4½" x 24½" outside border strips to sides. Press away from center block.

3. With right sides facing up, layer hemmed edges of backing pieces and overlap so that back measures 34½" x 24½" as shown. Baste pieces together along top and bottom edges where they overlap.

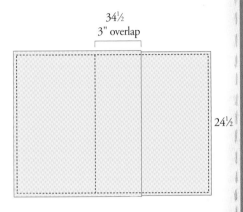

4. With right sides together, pin quilted sham top to backing. Sew all around outside edges with ¼"-wide seam. Trim corners, turn right side out, and press.

5. Refer to layout on page 10. Topstitch 3" from finished edge all around perimeter of sham as shown.

6. Insert pillow through opening in sham backing.

Small Pillow Covers

Use this smaller version of our Birdhouse Pillow Covers to create delightful decorative pillows for your bed. Finished size will be 20" x 18". Photo on cover.

FABRIC REQUIREMENTS

Follow fabric requirements for Birdhouse Pillow Covers Fabric A through Second Border.
Lining - ⅔ yard
Backing Panels - ⅜ yard
Pillow Form - 18"
Batting - 24" x 22"

CUTTING THE STRIPS AND PIECES

Follow cutting chart for Birdhouse Pillow Covers Fabric A through Second Border.
Lining
 One 24" x 22" piece
Back Panels
 Two 12½" x 18½"

BLOCK ASSEMBLY

1. You'll be making one birdhouse block following instructions beginning on page 11, steps one through five.

2. Sew 1½" x 16½" accent border strips to top and bottom of block. Press seams toward borders. Sew 1½" x 18½" accent border strips to sides. Press.

3. Sew 1½" x 18½" second border strips to sides. Press seams away from center block.

APPLIQUÉ

1. Trace appliqué design from page 37. Make template and use scrap to cut one of birdhouse hole #2. Cut out appliqué, adding ¼" seam allowance.

2. Machine stitch or refer to Hand Appliqué directions on page 110. Appliqué two 1¼" x 9½" roof pieces. Follow seam lines, and square ends as shown.

PILLOW ASSEMBLY

1. Layer batting between top and lining. Baste. Hand or machine quilt as desired. Trim batting and lining even with raw edge of pillow top.

2. Machine stitch ¼"-wide hem along one 18½" edge of each 12½" x 18½" back panel.

3. With right sides up, lay one backing piece over second piece so hemmed edges overlap, measuring 20½" x 18½". Adjust overlap to fit pillow top. Baste pieces together where they overlap.

4. With right sides together, position and pin pillow top to backing. Using ¼" seam, sew around edges. Trim corner, turn right side out, and press.

5. Top stitch between accent border and second border.

Beautiful Butterflies Wall Quilt

As softly colored *as the blossoms of spring, these delicate butterflies create a charming scene as they hover near their garden home.*

Constructed with a *variety of quick piecing techniques and completed with the simplest of appliqué and embroidery, they'll alight on your wall before you know it! Read all instructions before beginning and use ¼"-wide seams throughout.*

Beautiful Butterflies Wall Quilt
Finished Size: 40" x 41"
Photo: page 19

FABRIC REQUIREMENTS

Fabric A (Upper Wings) - eight scraps in a variety of colors

Fabric B (Background) - 1 yard

Fabric C (Lower Wings) - eight scraps in a variety of colors

Fabric D (Gable) - scrap

Fabrics E and F (Checkerboard) ⅛ yd of 2 contrasting fabrics

Fabric G (Gable Accent) - scrap

Fabric H (House Front) - scrap

Fabric I (Roof and Floor) - scraps

Appliqués - Assorted scraps for butterfly bodies and house openings

Inside Accent Border - ⅙ yard

Second Accent Border - ⅙ yard

Outside Border - ½ yard

Binding - ½ yard

Backing - 1¼ yards *

Lightweight Batting - 44" x 45" piece

Black Embroidery Floss or Perle Cotton

* Fabric must measure 45" wide.

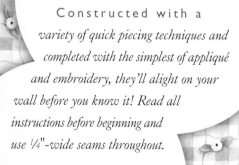

CUTTING THE STRIPS AND PIECES

Read first paragraph of Cutting the Strips and Pieces on page 7.

	FIRST CUT		SECOND CUT	
	Number of Strips or Pieces	Dimensions	Number of Pieces	Dimensions
FABRIC A eight fabrics	12	5½" squares *		
FABRIC B	5	1½" x 42"	50	1½" squares
			12	1½" x 5½"
			1	1½" x 11½"
			1	1½" x 10½"
			5	1½" x 6½"
	1	5½" x 42"	4	5½" squares
	2	3½" x 42"	8	3½" squares
			2	3½" x 10½"
			2	3" squares
	3	2½" x 42"	12	2½" squares
			5	2½" x 10½"
			1	2½" x 11½"
			2	2½" x 6½"
FABRIC C eight fabrics	4	3½" squares		
	8	3½" x 6½" **		
FABRIC D	1	3" x 5½"		
FABRICS E and F	1	1½" x 9" ea. (2 contrasting fabrics)		
FABRIC G	1	1" x 5½"		
FABRIC H	1	5½" square		
FABRIC I	1	1½" x 42"	1	1½" x 7½"
			2	1¼" x 6"
INSIDE ACCENT BORDER	4	1" x 42"		
SECOND ACCENT BORDER	4	1" x 42"		
OUTSIDE BORDER	4	3½" x 42"		
BINDING	5	2¾" x 42"		

* Cut two each from four fabrics, one each from four other fabrics.
** Cut four to match 3½" squares.

MAKING THE BLOCKS

In addition to the butterfly house, you will be making four full butterfly blocks and four butterfly profile blocks. Butterflies (bodies and wings) are made from a variety of scrap fabrics.

Whenever possible, use the Assembly Line Method on page 110.

Full Butterfly Blocks

1. Refer to Quick Corner Triangle directions on page 110. Sew 1½" Fabric B squares to two adjacent corners of one 5½" Fabric A square. Press. Make 4 matching pairs (a total of eight units).

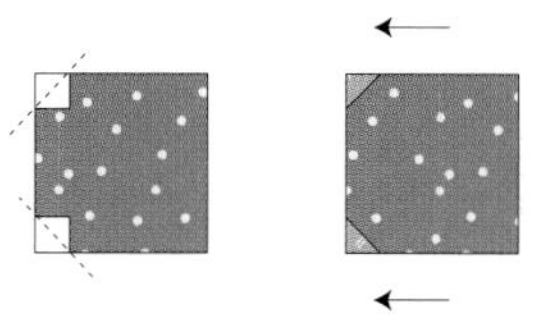

A = 5½ x 5½
B = 1½ x 1½
Make 4 matching pairs
(8 total units)

2. Sew one 2½" Fabric B square to each unit from step 1. Press. Make four of each variation shown, in matching fabric pairs.

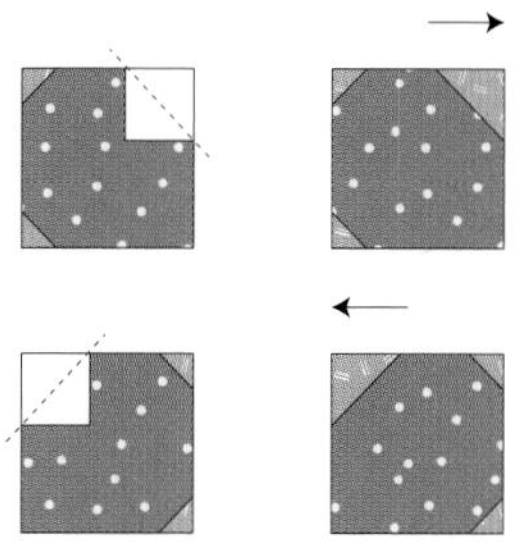

B = 2½ x 2½
Make 4 of each

3. Sew one 1½" x 5½" Fabric B piece to each unit from step 2. Press. Make four of each variation.

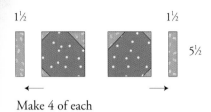

Make 4 of each

4. Sew 1½" Fabric B squares to two adjacent corners of each 3½" Fabric C square. Press. Make four.

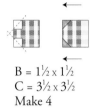

B = 1½ x 1½
C = 3½ x 3½
Make 4

5. Sew one 3½" Fabric B square to each unit from step 4. Press. Make four.

Make 4

6. Sew 1½" Fabric B squares to two adjacent corners on the short side of each of four 3½" x 6½" Fabric C strips. Match Fabric C pieces to Fabric C squares from step 4. Press. Make four.

B = 1½ x 1½
C = 3½ x 6½
Make 4

7. Sew matching colored units from step 5 and step 6 in pairs as shown. Press. Make four.

Make 4

8. Arrange one of each matching colored variation from step 3, one unit from step 7, and one 5½" Fabric B square as shown. Sew the units and squares into rows. Press. Sew the rows into blocks. Press. Make four blocks.

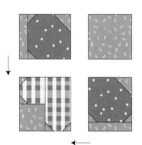

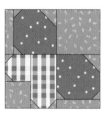

Block will measure 11½" square
Make 4

Butterfly Profile Blocks

1. Refer to Quick Corner Triangle directions on page 110. Sew 1½" Fabric B squares to two adjacent corners of remaining 5½" Fabric A squares. Press. Make two of each two variations labeling them Butterfly I and Butterfly II.

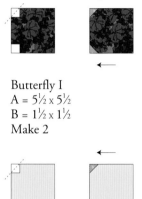

Butterfly I
A = 5½ x 5½
B = 1½ x 1½
Make 2

Butterfly II
A = 5½ x 5½
B = 1½ x 1½
Make 2

2. Sew one 2½" Fabric B square to each unit from step 1. Press. Make two of each variation.

Butterfly I
B = 2½ x 2½
Make 2

Butterfly II
B = 2½ x 2½
Make 2

3. Sew one 1½" x 5½" Fabric B piece to each unit from step 2. Press. Make two of each variation.

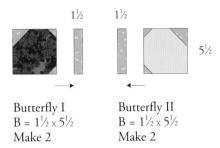

Butterfly I
B = 1½ x 5½
Make 2

Butterfly II
B = 1½ x 5½
Make 2

4. Sew 1½" Fabric B squares to two adjacent corners on one short side of remaining 3½" x 6½" Fabric C pieces. Press. Make two of each Fabric C color variation.

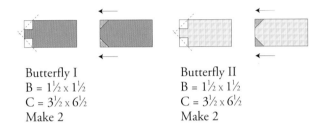

Butterfly I
B = 1½ x 1½
C = 3½ x 6½
Make 2

Butterfly II
B = 1½ x 1½
C = 3½ x 6½
Make 2

5. Sew one 3½" Fabric B square to each unit from step four. Press. Make two of each variation, labeling them Butterfly I and Butterfly II as shown.

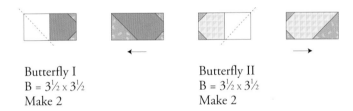

Butterfly I
B = 3½ x 3½
Make 2

Butterfly II
B = 3½ x 3½
Make 2

6. Sew units from step 3 and step 5 together, matching I and II variations as shown. Press. Make two of each block.

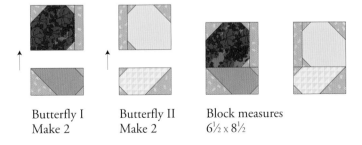

Butterfly I
Make 2

Butterfly II
Make 2

Block measures
6½ x 8½

Butterfly House Block
I. Refer to Quick Corner Triangle directions on page 110. Sew 3" Fabric B squares to 3" x 5½" Fabric D piece as shown. Press.

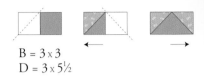

B = 3 x 3
D = 3 x 5½

2. Sew 1½" x 9" Fabric E and F strips together lengthwise. Press. Using rotary cutter and ruler, cut five 1½" segments from strip set. Arrange and sew segments to make checkerboard unit as shown. Press.

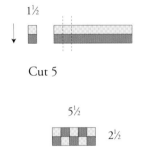

Cut 5

3. Refer to layout on page 14. Arrange and sew unit from step 1, 1" x 5½" Fabric G piece, 5½" Fabric H square, and checkerboard unit from step 3 in vertical row as shown. Press.

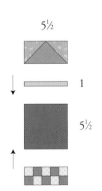

4. Sew unit from step 3 between two 2½" x 10½" Fabric B pieces. Press.

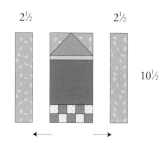

5. Sew 1½" x 7½" Fabric I piece between two 1½" Fabric B squares. Press.

6. Sew unit from step 4 to unit from step 5 as shown. Press.

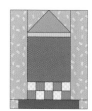

Block measures 9½ x 11½

ASSEMBLY

1. Sew two Butterfly Profile Blocks between 1½" x 6½" Fabric B pieces as shown. Press.

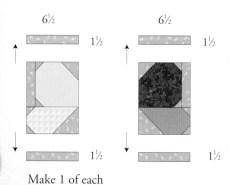

Make 1 of each

2. Sew Butterfly Profile Blocks from step 1 between one 2½" x 10½" Fabric B piece and one 3½" x 10½" Fabric B piece as shown. Press. Make one each.

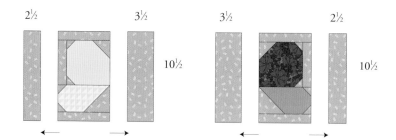

3. Refer to layout on page 14. Arrange each Butterfly Profile Block from step 2 between two full butterfly blocks in two vertical rows as shown. Sew the blocks together. Press.

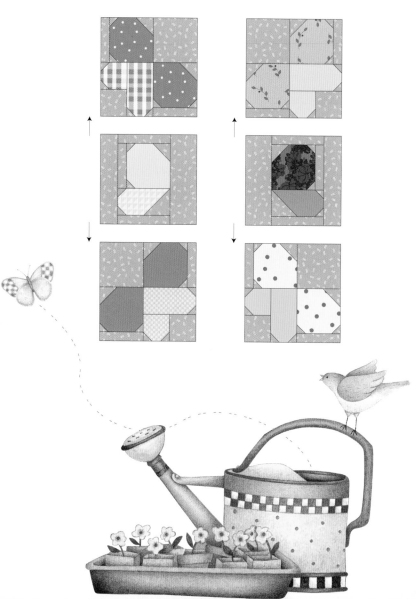

6. Sew remaining Butterfly II Profile Block between one 2½" x 6½" Fabric B piece and one 1½" x 6½" Fabric B piece as shown. Press.

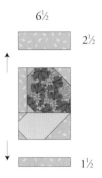

6½

2½

1½

7. Sew Butterfly II Profile Block from step 6 between one 1½" x 11½" Fabric B piece and one 2½ " x 11½" Fabric B piece as shown. Press.

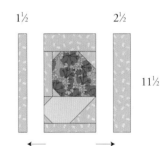

1½   2½

11½

4. Sew remaining Butterfly I Profile Block to one 2½" x 6½" Fabric B piece as shown. Press.

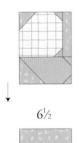

6½

2½

5. Sew Butterfly I Profile Block from step 4 between one 2½" x 10½" Fabric B piece and one 1½" x 10½" Fabric B piece as shown. Press.

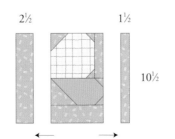

2½   1½

10½

8. Refer to layout on page 14. Arrange Butterfly House Block between Butterfly I Profile Block from step 5 and Butterfly II Profile Block from step 7 in a vertical row as shown. Sew the blocks together. Press.

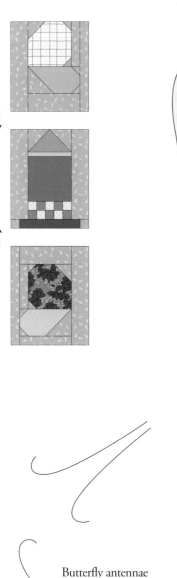

Butterfly antennae

APPLIQUÉ AND EMBROIDERY

1. Refer to Quick-Fuse Applique directions on page 111. Trace appliqué designs below. Use scraps to make eight of piece 1 (butterfly body) and three of piece 2 (house opening).

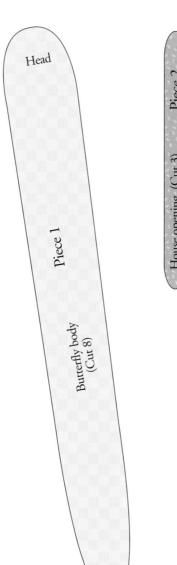

Head

Piece 1

Butterfly body
(Cut 8)

Piece 2

House opening (Cut 3)

2. Refer to layout on page 14. Position one butterfly body on each full and profile butterfly block as shown. Attach bodies to wings by fusing. Satin or blanket stitch appliqués by machine or hand to secure.

3. Referring to layout and color photo, appliqué three house openings on butterfly house as shown.

4. Referring to layout and color photo, appliqué two 1¼" x 6" Fabric I roof pieces on butterfly house. Follow the seam lines and square ends as shown.

5. Refer to Embroidery Stitch Guide on page 110. Use two strands of embroidery floss to stitch antennae with a running or stem stitch to each butterfly body.

BORDERS

1. Measure quilt through center from side to side. Trim two 1" x 42" inside accent border strips to this measurement. Sew to top and bottom. Press toward accent border.

2. Measure quilt through center from top to bottom, including border. Trim remaining 1" x 42" inside accent border strips to this measurement. Sew to sides. Press.

3. Repeat steps 1 and 2 to add 1" x 42" second accent border strips to top, bottom, and sides of quilt. Press.

4. Repeat steps 1 and 2 to add 3½" x 42" outside border strips to top, bottom, and sides of quilt. Press.

LAYERING AND FINISHING

1. Arrange and baste backing, batting, and top together referring to Layering the Quilt directions on page 111.

2. Hand or machine quilt as desired.

3. Refer to Binding the Quilt directions on page 111 and use the 2¾" x 42" binding strips to finish.

Beautiful Butterflies Twin-Size Quilt

For this quilt we suggest making twenty-four full butterfly blocks using six variations in color, and adding sashing between the blocks. Below are the fabric requirements. Finished size will be 59" x 85".

FABRIC REQUIREMENTS

Fabric A (Upper Wings) - ⅓ yard
  of six different fabrics
    Two 5½" x 42" strips
      Eight 5½" squares
    Repeat for *each* color

Fabric B (Background) - 2 yards
    Four 5½" x 42" strips
      Twenty-four 5½" squares
    Three 3½" x 42" strips
      Twenty-four 3½" squares
    Three 2½" x 42" strips
      Forty-eight 2½" squares
    Fifteen 1½" x 42" strips
      One hundred ninety-two
        1½" squares
      Forty-eight 1½" x 5½" pieces

Fabric C (Lower Wings) - ⅛ yard
  of six different fabrics
    One 3½" x 42" strip
      Four 3½" x 6½" pieces
      Four 3½" squares

Appliqués (Body) - ⅓ yard
    Cut twenty-four
Sashing - 1⅛ yards
    Thirteen 2½" x 42" strips
      Eighteen 2½" x 11½" pieces

Inside Accent Border - ⅓ yard
    Seven 1" x 42" strips

Second Accent Border - ⅓ yard
    Seven 1" x 42" strips

Outside Border - ⅞ yard
    Seven 3½" x 42" strips

Binding - ⅝ yard
    Seven 2¾" x 42" strips

Backing - 5⅛ yards

Lightweight Batting
    67" x 93" piece

Black Embroidery Floss or
    Perle Cotton

1. Refer to instructions for Full Butterfly Blocks in Beautiful Butterflies Wall Quilt on pages 15 and 16 to make four blocks of each color. Follow steps 1 through 8.

2. Arrange six horizontal rows of four blocks each. Place the 2½" x 11½" sashing pieces between the blocks in each horizontal row. Stitch together and press seams toward the sashing.

3. Cut five 12" strips from two 2½" x 42" strips and stitch to the five remaining 2½" x 42" strips. Trim to 2½" x 50½" and stitch between each horizontal row of blocks and sashing.

4. Refer to Applique and Embroidery (steps 1, 2, & 5), Borders, and Layering and Finishing instructions to complete quilt. Instead of trimming the border strips to fit the quilt, you will be stitching strips together to adjust measurements to the top you completed in step 3.

Butterfly House

Can't you just *picture this delightful domicile perched on your mantel or kitchen shelf? You'll feel as though it's springtime all year round!*

Check out the *numerous butterfly houses available at your local craft store. Choose a few to paint for yourself ... and a few extras to decorate for family and friends.*

Butterfly House

MATERIALS NEEDED

Unpainted butterfly house
Acrylic craft paints: dark brown,
 yellow, dark green, light green,
 medium blue, ivory, charcoal,
 and lavender for house;
 colors of choice for butterflies
Assorted paint brushes
Crackle medium

Scotch Magic™ Tape
Ruler
Tracing paper
Graphite transfer paper
Matte spray varnish
Antiquing medium
Stencil - ¼" checkerboard

PAINTING THE HOUSE

Refer to the color photo on page 22 for guidance as needed.

1. Paint roof with one coat of dark brown acrylic paint. Dry thoroughly.

2. Following manufacturer's directions, apply crackle medium to painted roof. Dry thoroughly.

3. Apply a quick, even coat of yellow paint to roof. Crackles will appear in painted surface. Do not touch, as surface is very fragile when wet. Dry thoroughly.

4. Apply one coat of dark green paint to door. Allow to dry thoroughly, then repeat steps 2 and 3 to apply crackle medium and topcoat of light green paint.

5. Apply two coats of same light green paint to rest of house.

6. Use a ¼" checkerboard stencil to apply checks with the dark green paint.

7. Paint base of house medium blue.

8. Measure 1" up from base of house, and mark guidelines in pencil. Apply strip of Scotch Magic™ Tape along guideline on all four sides of house. Paint area below tape with ivory paint. Leave tape in place for now.

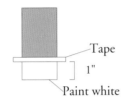

Tape

1"

Paint white

9. Measure and use ruler to mark two rows of ½" checks on ivory border. Paint every other check with charcoal paint in checkerboard fashion. Allow to dry throroughly and remove tape.

Tape

1"

10. Trace butterfly pattern below onto tracing paper. Position tracing paper on birdhouse front where you wish butterflies to appear. Tape in place, leaving one side open. Slide graphite paper under tracing paper, and use ballpoint pen to transfer design. Remove tape, tracing, and graphite paper.

11. Paint butterflies in colors of choice. Allow to dry thoroughly.

12. Apply a coat of matte spray varnish, and follow manufacturer's directions to apply antiquing medium to entire house. Finish with final coat of matte spray varnish.

Butterfly pattern

Blossoms & Butterflies Table Quilt

A wonderful whole-cloth, *patchwork print takes center stage in this soft-as-a-breeze springtime table topper. What could be faster, or more fuss-free?*

A striking butterfly *print frames it perfectly, while providing the source for the all-in-one machine stitched appliqués. Read all instructions before beginning, and use ¼"-wide seams throughout.*

Blossoms and Butterflies Table Quilt
Finished Size: 41½" square
Photo: page 25

FABRIC REQUIREMENTS

Center Panel - ⅝ yard
Inside Border - ⅛ yard
Corner Triangles - ½ yard
Accent Border - ¼ yard
Outside Border - 1 yard

Applique Butterfly Print - ¼ yard
Binding - ½ yard
Backing - 1⅜ yard *
Lightweight Batting - 46" square
*Fabric must measure 45" wide

CUTTING THE STRIPS AND PIECES

Read first paragraph of Cutting the Strips and Pieces on page 7.

		FIRST CUT		SECOND CUT	
		Number of Strips or pieces	Dimensions	Number of Pieces	Dimensions
	CENTER PANEL	1	17¼" square		
	INSIDE BORDER	2	1½" x 42"	2 2	1½" x 17¼" 1½" x 19¼"
	CORNER TRIANGLE	2	14¾" squares		
	ACCENT BORDER	4	1½" x 42"		
	OUTSIDE BORDER	4	6½" x 42"		
	BINDING	5	2¾" x 42"		

ASSEMBLY

1. Sew 1½" x 17¼" inside border strips to opposite sides of 17¼" center panel. Press toward border strips. Sew 1½" x 19¼" inside border strips to remaining sides. Press.

2. Cut each 14¾" square in half once diagonally to make four triangles. Sew one triangle to each side of unit from step 1. Press toward triangles. Square up quilt if necessary to measure 27" square.

3. Measure quilt through center from top to bottom. Cut two 1½" x 42" accent border strips to this measurement. Sew to sides. Press seams toward accent borders.

4. Measure quilt through center from side to side including borders. Cut remaining 1½" x 42" accent border strips to this measurement. Sew to top and bottom. Press.

5. Repeat steps 3 and 4 to fit, trim, and sew 6½"-wide outside borders to sides, top, and bottom of quilt. Press.

APPLIQUÉ

1. Referring to Quick-Fuse Appliqué directions on page 111, cut four butterfly motifs from butterfly print.

2. Refer to layout on page 24. Position and fuse one butterfly cut out in each corner triangle as shown.

3. Machine satin stitch or machine blanket stitch around butterflies.

LAYERING AND FINISHING

1. Layer backing, batting, and top together, referring to Layering the Quilt directions on page 111.

2. Machine or hand quilt as desired.

3. Cut one 2¾" x 42" binding strip into four equal pieces. Sew one piece to each remaining 2¾" x 42" strip. Refer to Binding the Quilt directions on page 111 to finish.

Summer

The good ol' summertime ... the flowers are bursting into bloom, the hot sunshine is smiling down upon us, and our feathered friends have nestled into their whimsical birdhouse homes to enjoy the summer season. And, of course, this inviting garden scene wouldn't be complete without those playful ladybugs adding their colorful charm.

Just sit back, relax, and bask in that warm, summertime glow. You'll have plenty of time to do just that ... and create touches of the season for your home, too, with our fast and easy projects.

Birdhouse Sampler Quilt

This friendly "neighborhood" adds a welcome touch to any room in your home! You'll have so much fun making this quilt, you'll want to use one or two of the patterns to make matching decorative pillows for your bed or favorite reading chair.

We've listed instructions for each block separately, so you can mix and match to your heart's content. Read all instructions before beginning and use ¼"-wide seams throughout.

Birdhouse Sampler Quilt
Finished Size: 51" x 71"
Photo: page 33

GENERAL FABRIC REQUIREMENTS

Fabrics for individual houses are listed with those blocks

Fabric A (Background) - ¾ yard of two different fabrics
Birdhouse Holes - Scraps
Block Frame - ⅝ yard

Corner Squares - ⅛ yard
Sashing and Inside Border - ¾ yard
Outside Border - ⅞ yard
Binding - ⅝ yard
Backing - 3⅛ yards
Lightweight Batting - 53" x 73" piece

28

GENERAL CUTTING THE STRIPS AND PIECES

Read first paragraph of Cutting the Strips and Pieces on page 7.

		FIRST CUT		SECOND CUT	
		Number of Strips	Dimensions	Number of Pieces	Dimensions
	FABRIC A	See individual blocks			
	BLOCK FRAME	12	1½" x 42"	24	1½" x 16½"
	CORNER SQUARES	1	1½" x 42"	24	1½" square
	SASHING	4	2½" x 42"	8	2½" x 18½"
	INSIDE BORDER	5	2½" x 42"		
	OUTSIDE BORDER	6	4½" x 42"		
	BINDING	7	2¾" x 42"		

Summer ~ *Birdhouse Sampler Quilt*

MAKING THE BLOCKS

Whenever possible, use the Assembly Line Method on page 110. Press in direction of arrows in diagrams.

BUNGALOW BIRDHOUSE BLOCK	Number of Pieces	Dimensions
FABRIC REQUIREMENTS		FIRST CUT
FABRIC A (background) — ⅛ yard	2	2½" x 9½"
	2	1½" x 6½"
	2	1½" x 6"
	2	1½" x 5½"
	2	1½" squares
FABRIC B (upper house) — ⅛ yard	1	3½" x 2"
	4	1½" x 4"
	1	1½" x 12½"
	4	1½" squares
FABRIC C (windows) — scraps	2	3" x 4"
FABRIC D (window boxes) — scraps	2	1½" x 5"
FABRIC E (lower house & tower) — scraps	2	5" x 4"
	1	3½" x 2½"
FABRIC F (door) — scrap	1	3½" x 7"
FABRIC G (roof) — ⅛ yard	1	3½" x 14½"
	2	1½" x 6"
	1	1½" x 4½"
FABRIC H (base) — ⅛ yard	1	1½" x 16½"

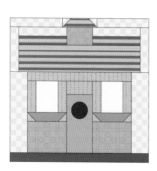

Bungalow Birdhouse Block
Block measures 16½" x 16½"

BLOCK ASSEMBLY

1. Sew each 3" x 4" Fabric C piece between two 1½" x 4" Fabric B pieces. Press. Make two.

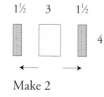

Make 2

2. Refer to Quick Corner Triangle directions on page 110. Sew two 1½" Fabric B squares to each 1½" x 5" Fabric D piece as shown. Press. Make two.

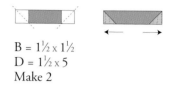

B = 1½ x 1½
D = 1½ x 5
Make 2

3. Sew each unit from step 2 between one unit from step 1 and one 5" x 4" Fabric E piece as shown. Press. Make two.

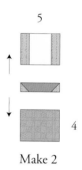

Make 2

4. Sew 3½" x 2" Fabric B piece to 3½" x 7" Fabric F piece as shown. Press.

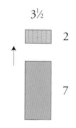

5. Sew unit from step 4 between two units from step 3. Press.

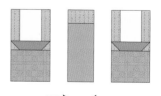

6. Sew 1½" x 12½" Fabric B piece to unit from step 5 as shown. Press.

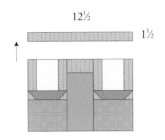

12½

1½

7. Sew unit from step 6 between two 2½" x 9½" Fabric A pieces. Press.

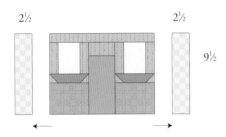

2½   2½

9½

8. Sew 1½" x 6" Fabric A piece to each 1½" x 6" Fabric G piece.

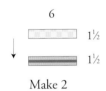

6

1½

1½

Make 2

9. Sew 3½" x 2½" Fabric E piece between units from step 8. Press.

6   3½   6

2½

10. Sew unit from step 9 to 3½" x 14½" Fabric G strip as shown. Press.

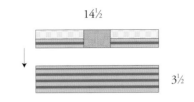

14½

3½

11. Sew unit from step 10 between two 1½" x 5½" Fabric A pieces. Press.

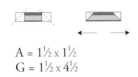

1½   1½

5½

12. Refer to Quick Corner Triangle directions. Sew two 1½" Fabric A squares to 1½" x 4½" Fabric G piece as shown. Press.

A = 1½ x 1½
G = 1½ x 4½

13. Sew unit from step 12 between two 1½" x 6½" Fabric A pieces. Press.

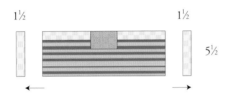

6½   6½

1½

14. Sew unit from step 13 to unit from step 11 as shown. Press.

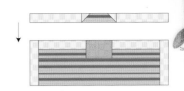

15. Refer to layout on page 30 and color photo on page 33. Sew unit from step 7 between unit from step 14 and 1½" x 16½" Fabric H strip. Press toward bottom edge of block.

16. Trace appliqué design from page 37. Make template and use scrap to cut one birdhouse hole #2. Cut out appliqué, adding ¼" seam allowance. Machine stitch or refer to Hand Appliqué directions on page 110 to appliqué birdhouse hole on door.

31

VINE STREET BIRDHOUSE BLOCK		Number of Pieces	Dimensions
	FABRIC REQUIREMENTS		FIRST CUT
FABRIC A (background)	⅓ yard	2 2 2	3½" x 8½" 3½" x 6½" 5½" squares
FABRIC B (pillars & upper roof appliqués)	scraps	2 2	1½" x 5½" 1¼" x 9"
FABRIC C (door)	scrap	1	2½" x 5½"
FABRIC D (lower house)	scraps	2 2	3½" x 6½" 1½" squares
FABRIC E (lower roof)	scrap	1	4½" x 1½"
FABRIC F (upper house)	¼ yard	1 2 1	6½" x 10½" 2" x 2½" 5½" x 2½"
FABRIC G (windows)	scraps	2	1½" x 2½"
FABRIC H (base)	⅛ yard	1	2½" x 16½"

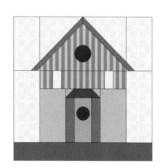

Vine Street Birdhouse Block

Block measures 16½" x 16½"

BLOCK ASSEMBLY

1. Sew 2½" x 5½" Fabric C piece between two 1½" x 5½" Fabric B pieces. Press.

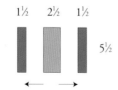

1½   2½   1½

5½

2. Refer to Quick Corner Triangle directions on page 110. Sew two 1½" Fabric D squares to 4½" x 1½" Fabric E piece as shown. Press.

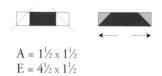

A = 1½ x 1½
E = 4½ x 1½

3. Sew unit from step 2 to unit from step 1 as shown. Press.

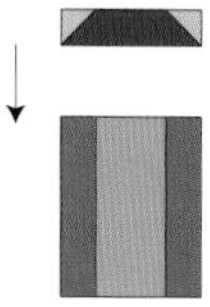

4. Sew unit from step 3 between two 3½" x 6½" Fabric D pieces. Press.

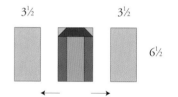

3½   3½

6½

5. Arrange and sew two 2" x 2½" Fabric F pieces, two 1½" x2½" Fabric G pieces, and one 5½" x 2½" Fabric F piece in order shown to make a horizontal row. Press.

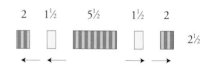

2   1½   5½   1½   2

2½

6. Sew unit from step 5 to unit from step 4. Press.

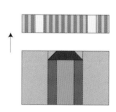

7. Sew unit from step 6 between two 3½" x 8½" Fabric A pieces. Press.

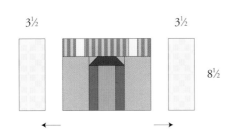

8. Refer to Quick Corner Triangle directions on page 110. Sew two 5½" Fabric A squares to 6½" x 10½" Fabric F piece as shown. Press.

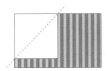 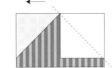

A = 5½ x 5½
F = 6½ x 10½

9. Sew unit from step 8 between two 3½" x 6½" Fabric A pieces. Press.

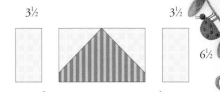

10. Refer to layout on page 32 and color photo. Sew unit from step 7 between unit from step 9 and 2½" x 16½" Fabric H strip. Press toward bottom edge of block.

11. Trace appliqué designs from page 37. Make templates and use scraps to cut one each of birdhouse hole #1 and #2. Cut out appliqués, adding ¼" seam allowance.

12. Machine stitch or refer to Hand Appliqué directions on page 110. Appliqué two 1¼" x 9" Fabric B roof pieces over roof. Follow seam lines, and square ends as shown. Refer to layout on page 32 and color photo to appliqué birdhouse hole #2 on upper house, and birdhouse hole #1 on door.

PICKET FENCE BIRDHOUSE BLOCK		Number of Pieces	Dimensions
	FABRIC REQUIREMENTS		**FIRST CUT**
FABRIC A (background)	¼ yard	2 2 2	6½" squares 2½" x 6½" 3½" x 9½"
FABRIC B (fence)	⅛ yard	5 2	1½" x 3½" 1" x 10½"
FABRIC C (lower house)	¼ yard	1 1	5" x 10½" 1½" x 10½"
FABRIC D (house trim)	⅛ yard	1	1" x 10½"
FABRIC E (middle house)	⅛ yard	1	2½" x 10½"
FABRIC F (upper house)	¼ yard	2	6½" squares
FABRIC G (base)	⅛ yard	1	1½" x 16½"
ROOF APPLIQUÉS	⅛ yard	2	1¼" x 9"

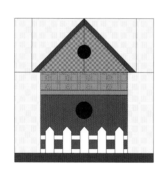

Picket Fence Birdhouse Block

Block measures 16½" x 16½"

BLOCK ASSEMBLY

1. Fold 1½" x 3½" Fabric B piece in half lengthwise with right sides together. Using ¼" seam, stitch across top edge of each piece. Turn sewn pieces right side out. Press point at top, then turn under ¼" seam allowance on long sides and press. Make five.

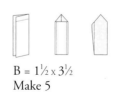

B = 1½ x 3½
Make 5

2. Sew 5" x 10½" Fabric C piece, one 1" x 10½" Fabric B piece, 1½"x 10½" Fabric C piece, and remaining 1" x 10½" Fabric B piece together as shown. Press.

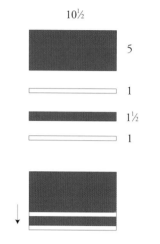

10½

5

1

1½

1

3. Refer to layout on this page and color photo on page 33. Machine stitch or refer to Hand Appliqué directions on page 110 to appliqué fence posts from step 1 to unit from step 2.

4. Sew 1" x 10½" Fabric D piece between 2½" x 10½" Fabric E piece and unit from step 3. Press.

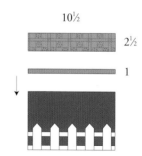

10½

2½

1

5. Sew unit from step 4 between two 3½" x 9½" Fabric A pieces. Press.

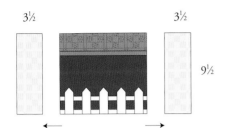

3½   3½

9½

6. Refer to Quick Corner Triangle directions on page 110. Sew 6½" Fabric A and 6½" Fabric F squares together in pairs. Press. Make two.

A = 6½ x 6½
F = 6½ x 6½
Make 2

7. Arrange and sew two 2½" x 6½" Fabric A pieces and units from step 6 to make a horizontal row as shown. Press.

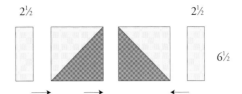

2½   2½

6½

8. Refer to layout on page 34 and color photo on page 33. Sew unit from step 5 between unit from step 7, and 1½" x 16½" Fabric G strip. Press toward bottom edge of block.

9. Trace appliqué designs from page 37. Make templates and use scraps to cut one each of birdhouse hole #1 and #2. Cut out appliqués, adding ¼" seam allowance.

10. Machine stitch or refer to Hand Appliqué directions on page 110. Appliqué two 1¼" x 9" roof pieces over roof. Follow seam lines, and square ends as shown. Refer to layout on page 34 and color photo on page 33 to appliqué birdhouse holes on upper house and lower house as shown.

SUNSET BIRDHOUSE BLOCK		Number of Pieces	Dimensions
	FABRIC REQUIREMENTS		FIRST CUT
FABRIC A (background)	¼ yard	2 2 2 2	8½" squares 3½" squares 3" x 2" 2" x 6"
FABRIC B (lower house)	⅛ yard	1	3½" x 13½"
FABRIC C (upper house & trim #1)	¼ yard	1 1 1	8½" x 16½" 1½" x 13½" 1" x 13½"
FABRIC D (trim #2)	⅛ yard	1	1½" x 13½"
FABRIC E (birdhouse base & roof appliqués)	⅛ yard	1 2	2" x 11½" 1⅝" x 11¾"
FABRIC F (base #2)	⅛ yard	1	1½" x 16½"

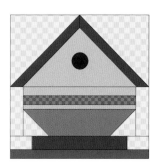

Sunset
Birdhouse Block
Block measures 16½" x 16½"

BLOCK ASSEMBLY

1. Refer to Quick Corner Triangle directions on page 110. Sew two 3½" Fabric A squares to 3½" x 13½" Fabric B strip as shown. Press.

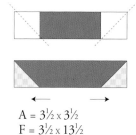

A = 3½ x 3½
F = 3½ x 13½

2. Arrange and sew 1½" x 13½" Fabric C strip, 1½" x 13½" Fabric D strip, 1" x 13½" Fabric C strip, and unit from step 1 to make a vertical row as shown. Press.

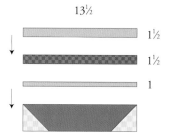

13½

1½
1½
1

3. Sew unit from step 2 between two 2" x 6" Fabric A pieces. Press.

2   2

6

4. Refer to Quick Corner Triangle directions on page 110. Sew two 8½" Fabric A squares to 8½" x 16½" Fabric C strip as shown. Press.

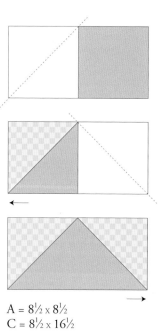

A = 8½ x 8½
C = 8½ x 16½

5. Sew 2" x 11½" Fabric E piece between two 3" x 2" Fabric A pieces as shown. Press.

6. Refer to layout on page 36 and color photo. Arrange and sew unit from step 4, unit from step 3, unit from step 5, and 1½" x 16½" Fabric F strip to make a vertical row. Press.

7. Trace appliqué designs. Make template and use scrap to cut one birdhouse hole #2. Cut out appliqué, adding ¼" seam allowance.

8. Machine stitch or refer to Hand Appliqué directions on page 110. Appliqué two 1⅝" x 11¾" Fabric E pieces over roof. Follow seam lines, and square ends as shown. Refer to layout on page 36 and color photo to appliqué birdhouse hole on upper house as shown.

Make finished size 1⅝"

#2

Birdhouse Holes
(only two sizes required
for entire quilt)

Make finished size 1¼"

#1

SCHOOLHOUSE BIRDHOUSE BLOCK		Number of Pieces	Dimensions
	FABRIC REQUIREMENTS		FIRST CUT
FABRIC A (background)	¼ yard	2 2 2	7½" square 1½" x 7½" 2½" x 7½"
FABRIC B (small gable)	scrap	1	4½" x 3½"
FABRIC C (large gable)	⅛ yard	2 1 2	5½" x 3½" 3½" x 14½" 2½" square
FABRIC D (schoolhouse trim)	⅛ yard	1	1½" x 14½"
FABRIC E (roof appliqués)	⅛ yard	2 2	1¼" x 10½" 1" x 4½"
FABRIC F (windows)	scraps	2	2½" x 4"
FABRIC G (schoolhouse front)	⅙ yard	4 4 1	2½" x 1½" 1¾" x 6" 3½" x 2"
FABRIC H (lower wall)	scrap	2	2" x 5"
FABRIC I (door)	scrap	1	3½" x 6"
FABRIC J (base)	⅛ yard	2 2	1½" x 7" 1½" x 6½"
FABRIC K (steps)	scraps	1 1	1½" x 3½" 1½" x 4½"

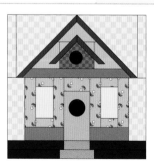

Schoolhouse Birdhouse Block

Block measures 16½" x 16½"

BLOCK ASSEMBLY

1. Refer to Quick Corner Triangle directions on page 110. Sew two 2½" Fabric C squares to 4½" x 3½" Fabric B piece as shown. Press.

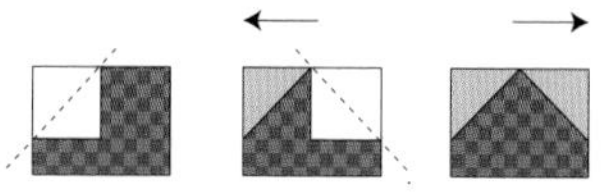

B = 4½ x 3½
C = 2½ x 2½

2. Sew unit from step 1 between two 5½" x 3½" Fabric C pieces. Press.

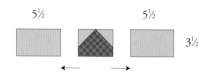

5½   5½

3½

3. Sew unit from step 2 between 3½" x 14½" Fabric C strip and 1½" x 14½" Fabric D strip. Press.

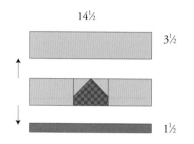

14½

3½

1½

4. Refer to Quick Corner Triangle directions on page 110. Sew two 7½" Fabric A squares to unit from step 3 as shown. Press.

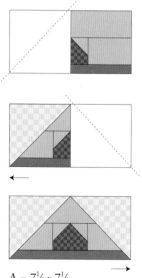

A = 7½ x 7½

5. Sew unit from step 4 between two 1½" x 7½" Fabric A pieces. Press.

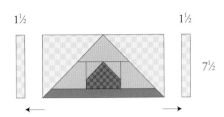

6. Sew two 2½" x 1½" Fabric G pieces to each 2½" x 4" Fabric F piece as shown. Press. Make two.

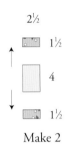

Make 2

7. Sew each unit from step 6 between two 1¾" x 6" Fabric G pieces as shown. Press. Make two.

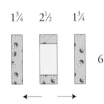

8. Sew one 2" x 5" Fabric H piece to each unit from step 7 as shown. Press. Make two.

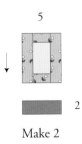

Make 2

9. Sew 3½" x 2" Fabric G piece to 3½" x 6" Fabric I piece as shown. Press.

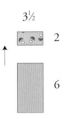

10. Arrange and sew two 2½" x 7½" Fabric A pieces, two units from step 8, and unit from step 9 to make a horizontal row as shown. Press.

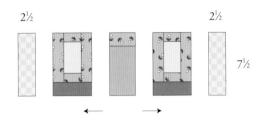

11. Sew 1½" x 3½" Fabric K piece between two 1½" x 7" Fabric J pieces. Label this Row A, and press. Repeat to sew 1½" x 4½" Fabric K piece between two 1½" x 6½" Fabric J pieces. Label this Row B, and press.

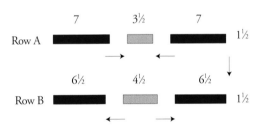

12. Refer to layout on page 38 and color photo on page 33. Arrange and sew unit from step 5, unit from step 10, and rows A and B from step 11. Press toward bottom edge of block.

13. Trace appliqué designs from page 37. Make templates and use scraps to cut one each of birdhouse hole #1 and #2. Cut out appliqués, adding ¼" seam allowance.

14. Refer to layout on page 38 and color photo on page 33. Machine stitch or refer to Hand Appliqué directions on page 110. Appliqué two 1¼" x 10½" Fabric E roof pieces over large gable and two 1" x 4½" Fabric E roof pieces over small gable. Follow seam lines, and square ends as shown. Appliqué birdhouse hole #1 to small gable and birdhouse hole #2 to door.

THREE'S COMPANY BIRDHOUSE BLOCK

THREE'S COMPANY BIRDHOUSE BLOCK		Number of Pieces	Dimensions
	FABRIC REQUIREMENTS		FIRST CUT
FABRIC A (background)	⅙ yard	2 2 4	2" x 8" 2" squares 4½" squares
FABRIC B (lower house)	¼ yard	1 1 2	13½" x 5" 13½" x 2½" 2½" x 1½"
FABRIC C (perch & roof appliqués)	⅛ yard	1 2 2 2	1½" x 9½" 1¼" x 6½" 1¼" x 4½" 1¼" x 2½"
FABRIC D (upper house)	¼ yard	1 2	8½" x 6" 4½" x 2"
FABRIC E (birdhouse base #1)	⅛ yard	1	1½" x 16½"
FABRIC F (birdhouse base #2)	⅛ yard	1	2½" x 16½"
STAR APPLIQUÉ	scrap	1	5" square

Three's Company Birdhouse Block

Block measures 16½" x 16½"

BLOCK ASSEMBLY

1. Sew 1½" x 9½" Fabric C piece between two 2½" x 1½" Fabric B pieces as shown. Press.

2½"   9½"   2½"   1½"

2. Sew unit from step 1 between 13½" x 5" Fabric B strip and 13½" x 2½" Fabric B strip. Press.

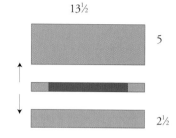

13½

5

2½

3. Sew unit from step 2 between two 2" x 8" Fabric A pieces. Press.

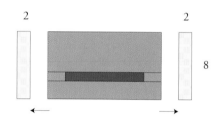

2   2

8

4. Refer to Quick Corner Triangle directions on page 110. Sew two 4½" Fabric A squares to 8½" x 6" Fabric D piece as shown. Press.

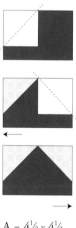

A = 4½ x 4½
D = 8½ x 6

5. Refer to Quick Corner Triangle directions on page 110. Sew one 2" Fabric A square to each 4½" x 2" Fabric D piece as shown. Press. Make one of each.

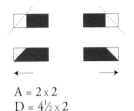

A = 2 x 2
D = 4½ x 2
Make 1 of each

6. Sew remaining 4½" Fabric A squares to each unit from step 5 as shown. Press. Make one of each.

4½
4½

Make 1 of each

7. Sew unit from step 4 between units from step 6 as shown. Press.

8. Refer to layout on page 40 and color photo on page 33. Arrange and sew unit from step 7, unit from step 3, 1½" x 16½" Fabric E strip, and 2¼" x 16½" Fabric F strip to make a vertical row. Press toward bottom edge of block.

9. Trace appliqué designs from page 37 and below. Make templates and use scraps to cut one star and three of birdhouse hole #2. Cut out appliqués, adding ¼" seam allowance.

10. Refer to layout on page 40 and color photo on page 33. Machine stitch or refer to Hand Appliqué directions on page 110. Appliqué two 1¼" x 6½", two 1¼" x 4½", and two 1¼" x 2½" Fabric C roof pieces over roof line. Follow seam lines, and square ends as shown. Appliqué three of birdhouse hole #2 to lower house, and star to upper house.

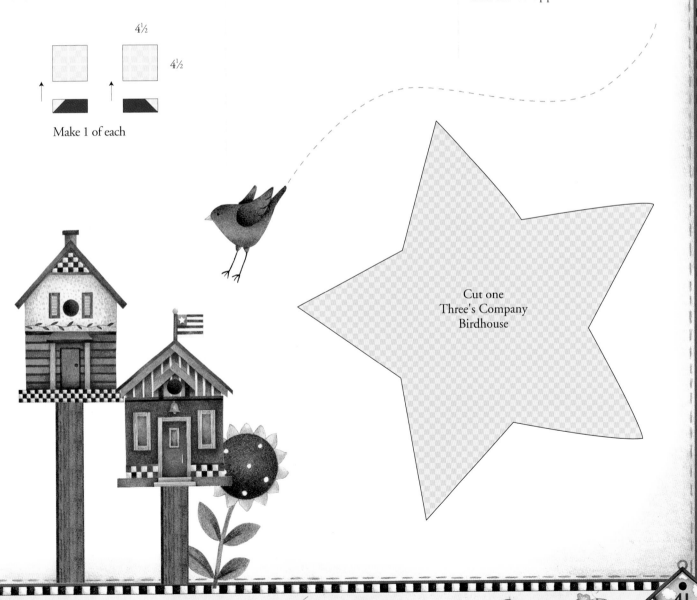

Cut one
Three's Company
Birdhouse

BIRDHOUSE SAMPLER QUILT ASSEMBLY

1. Sew 1½" x 16½" framing strips to top and bottom of each birdhouse block. Press toward framing strips.

2. Sew each remaining 1½" x 16½" framing strip between two 1½" corner squares. Press toward framing strips.

3. Sew unit from step 2 to sides of each birdhouse block. Press away from block.

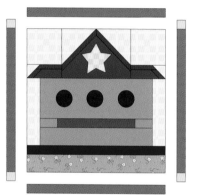

Corner square = 1½ x 1½
Frame = 1½ x 16½

4. Refer to layout on page 28 and color photo on page 33. Arrange three birdhouse blocks and four 2½" x 18½" sashing strips in a vertical row. Sew, then press toward sashing strips. Make two rows.

5. Sew 2½" x 42" sashing strips together in pairs. Measure quilt through center from top to bottom, and trim sewn strips to this measurement.

6. Refer to layout on page 28 and color photo on page 33. Arrange the two birdhouse rows from step 1 and the three sashing strips from step 5, alternating them. Sew sashing and rows together. Press toward sashing strips.

7. Sew 4½" x 42" border strips end to end to make one continuous 4½"-wide strip. Measure quilt through center from side to side. Trim two 4½"-wide border strips to this measurement. Sew to top and bottom. Press toward border strips.

8. Measure quilt through center from top to bottom including borders just added. Trim two 4½"-wide strips to this measurement. Sew to sides and press.

LAYERING AND FINISHING

1. Cut backing crosswise into two equal pieces. Sew pieces together on the long edges to make one 56" x 84" (approximate) backing piece. Arrange and baste backing, batting, and top together referring to Layering the Quilt directions on page 111.

2. Hand or machine quilt as desired.

3. Cut one 2¾" x 42" binding strip in half and sew halves to two remaining 2¾" x 42" strips. Sew remaining 2¾" x 42" binding strips together in pairs. Using shorter strips for top and bottom and longer strips for sides, refer to Binding the Quilt directions on page 111 to finish.

Sunset Birdhouse Table Runner

Bring the tender glow of a summertime sunset to your table with this quick and easy table runner.

Finished size will be 17" x 63".

FABRIC REQUIREMENTS

Sunset Birdhouse Block - see fabric requirements page 36.
Triangle/ends - ⅜ yard cut into
  Two 3½" x 16½" pieces
  One 12¼" square cut once diagonally

Background - ¼ yard cut into
  One 7½" x 16½" piece
Binding - ⅜ yard cut into
  Four 2¾" x 42" pieces
Backing - 1 yard

ASSEMBLY

1. Construct two Sunset Birdhouse Blocks following instructions beginning on page 36. Option: Make several table runners using different Sampler Birdhouse blocks for different rooms of your house.

2. Sew 7½" x 16½" background fabric between two Sunset Birdhouse Blocks.

3. Sew unit from step 2 between two 3½" x 16½" end pieces.

4. Cut 12¼" square once diagonally and sew triangles to the end pieces.

5. Quick fuse or hand appliqué flowers onto end pieces. Flower templates are found on page 49 in Chapel Birdhouse Wallhanging.

LAYERING AND FINISHING

1. Cut backing fabric lengthwise into two equal pieces. Sew pieces together to make one 22" x 72" (approximately) backing piece. Arrange and baste backing, batting, and top together, referring to Layering the Quilt directions on page 111.

2. Hand or machine quilt as desired. Trim batting ¼" from raw edge of table runner.

3. Sew 2¾" binding strips together end to end to make one continuous 2¾" strip. From this strip cut two 48" strips, and four 14" strips.

4. Sew binding following instructions on page 82 for Falling Leaves Table Runner, Layering and Finishing steps 3 through 6.

Garden Chapel Wallhanging

June is the
month for weddings, and what summertime (or anytime) bride wouldn't be thrilled with this feminine, fanciful, flower-bedecked wallhanging?

How about using
it to decorate at the wedding shower or reception, then present it afterward to the happy couple? No wedding on the horizon? It will be perfect at a garden party or afternoon tea, too. Read all instructions before beginning and use ¼"-wide seams throughout.

Garden Chapel Wallhanging
Finished Quilt Size: 23" x 39"
Photo: page 47

FABRIC REQUIREMENTS

Fabric A (Door) - Scrap
Fabric B (Hedges) - Scraps
Fabric C (Center Wall) - ⅙ yard
Fabric D (Outside Walls) - ⅛ yard
Fabric E (Trim #1) - Scraps
Fabric F (Trim #2) - Scraps
Fabric G (Background) - ½ yard
Fabric H (House Base, Inside, and
  Outside Borders) - ⅓ yard
Fabric I (Post) - ⅛ yard
Fabric J (Upper Wall)-Scrap

Corners - Scraps
Middle Border - ¼ yard
Roof and Birdhouse Hole
  Appliqués - Scraps
Flower, Stem, and Leaf Appliqués -
  Assorted red, yellow, and
  green scraps
Binding - ⅜ yard
Backing - 1¼ yards
Lightweight Batting - 27" x 43" piece

44

CUTTING THE STRIPS AND PIECES

Read first paragraph of Cutting the Strips and Pieces on page 7.

		FIRST CUT		SECOND CUT	
		Number of Strips or Pieces	Dimensions	Number of Pieces	Dimensions
	FABRIC A	1	2½" x 7½"		
	FABRIC B	2	1" x 7½"		
	FABRIC C	1	6½" x 2½"		
		1	2" x 42"	2	2" squares
				2	2" x 6½"
		1	1½" x 3½"		
	FABRIC D	2	2½" x 6½"		
		2	3½" squares		
	FABRIC E	2	1" x 4"		
	FABRIC F	2	2" x 4"		
		1	1" x 6½"		
	FABRIC G	1	6½" x 42"	1	6½" x 1½"
				2	6½" x 12½"
				2	4½" x 6½"
		2	4½" x 3½"		
		2	3½" squares		
		2	2½" x 8½"		
		2	1½" squares		
	FABRIC H	6	1½" x 42"	2	1½" x 36½"
				2	1½" x 30½"
				2	1½" x 20½"
				2	1½" x 14½"
				1	1½" x 12½"
	FABRIC I	1	2½" x 12½"		
	FABRIC J	1	6½" x 6"		
	CORNERS	8	1½" squares		
	MIDDLE BORDER	3	2½" x 42"	2	2½" x 16½"
				2	2½" x 36½"
	ROOF APPLIQUÉS	1	1" x 42"	2	1" x 6"
				2	1" x 4½"
				2	1" x 3"
	BINDING	4	2¾" x 42"		

MAKING THE CENTER PANEL

For the center panel, you'll be making one birdhouse block, complete with base, post, and appliquéd flowers. Whenever possible, use the Assembly Line Method on page 110. Press in direction of arrows.

1. Sew 2½" x 7½" Fabric A piece between two 1" x 7½" Fabric B pieces. Press.

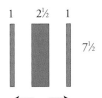

2. Refer to Quick Corner Triangle directions on page 110. Sew 2" Fabric C squares to unit from step 1 as shown. Press.

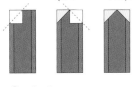

C = 2 x 2

3. Sew 1½" x 3½" Fabric C piece and unit from step 2 as shown. Press.

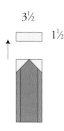

4. Sew one 2" x 6½" Fabric C piece to each 2½" x 6½" Fabric D piece as shown. Press. Make two.

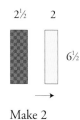

Make 2

5. Sew one 1" x 4" Fabric E piece to each 2" x 4" Fabric F piece as shown. Press. Make two.

Make 2

6. Sew one unit from step 5 to each unit from step 4 as shown. Press.

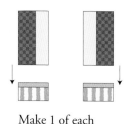

Make 1 of each

7. Arrange and sew two 2½" x 8½" Fabric G pieces, both units from step 6, and unit from step 3 in order shown to make a horizontal row. Press.

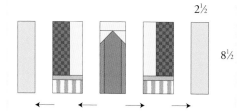

8. Refer to Quick Corner Triangle directions on page 110. Sew 3½" Fabric G squares to 6½" x 6" Fabric J piece as shown. Press.

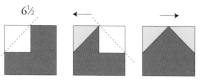

D = 6½ x 6
G = 3½ x 3½

9. Arrange and sew 6½" x 1½" Fabric G piece, unit from step 8, 1" x 6½" Fabric F piece, and 6½" x 2½" Fabric C piece in order shown to make a vertical row. Press.

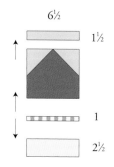

10. Refer to Quick Corner Triangle directions on page 110. Sew one 3½" Fabric D square to each 4½" x 3½" Fabric G piece as shown. Press. Make one of each.

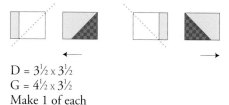

D = 3½ x 3½
G = 4½ x 3½
Make 1 of each

11. Sew one 4½" x 6½" Fabric G piece to each unit from step 10 as shown. Press. Make one of each.

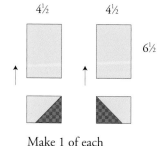

Make 1 of each

Debbie Mumm's® Birdhouses for Every Season

12. Sew unit from step 9 between units from step 11 as shown. Press.

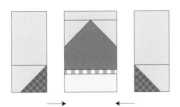

13. Sew unit from step 12 to unit from step 7 as shown. Press.

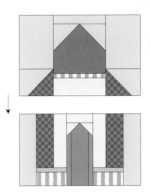

14. Sew 1½" x 12½" Fabric H piece between two 1½" Fabric G squares. Press.

15. Sew 2½" x 12½" Fabric I piece between two 6½" x 12½" Fabric G pieces. Press.

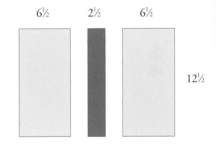

16. Refer to layout on page 44 and color photo on page 47. Arrange and sew units from steps 13, 14, and 15 in order shown to make a vertical row and complete center panel.

APPLIQUÉ

1. Trace appliqué designs. Make templates and use scraps to cut one upper and one lower birdhouse hole. Cut out appliqués, adding ¼" seam allowance.

2. Machine stitch or refer to Hand Appliqué on page 110. Appliqué upper birdhouse hole to birdhouse gable, and lower birdhouse hole to birdhouse door. Appliqué two 1" x 6" roof pieces over gable, two 1" x 4½" roof pieces over secondary roof line, and two 1" x 3" roof pieces over door. Follow seam lines, and square ends as shown. Refer to layout on page 44 and color photo on page 47 for guidance as needed.

3. Trace flower appliqué designs. Make templates and use scraps to trace one each of pieces 1 through 24. Cut out appliqués, adding ¼" seam allowance around each piece.

4. Referring to layout on page 44, and color photo on page 47, position appliqués around birdhouse post. Use your preferred method to stitch appliqués in place.

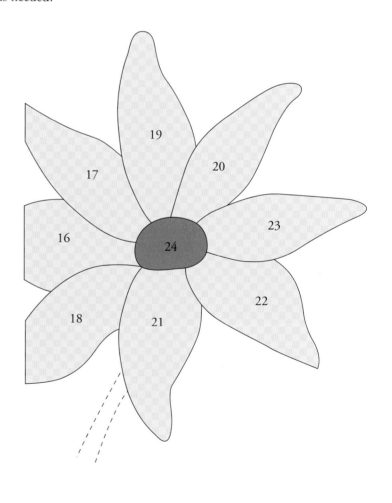

ASSEMBLY

1. Sew 1½" x 14½" Fabric H inside border strips to top and bottom of center panel. Press toward border strips.

2. Sew 1½" corner squares to short ends of each 1½" x 30½" Fabric H inside border strip. Press toward border strips. Sew strips to sides. Press.

3. Sew 2½" x 16½" middle border strips to top and bottom. Press toward middle borders.

4. Sew 2½" x 36½" middle border strips to sides. Press.

5. Sew 1½" x 20½" Fabric H outside border strips to top and bottom. Press.

6. Sew remaining 1½" corner squares to short ends of each 1½" x 36½" Fabric H outside border strip. Sew strips to sides. Press.

LAYERING AND FINISHING

1. Arrange and baste backing, batting, and top together referring to Layering the Quilt directions on page 111.

2. Hand or machine quilt as desired.

3. Refer to Binding the Quilt directions on page 111, and use 2¾" x 42" strips to finish.

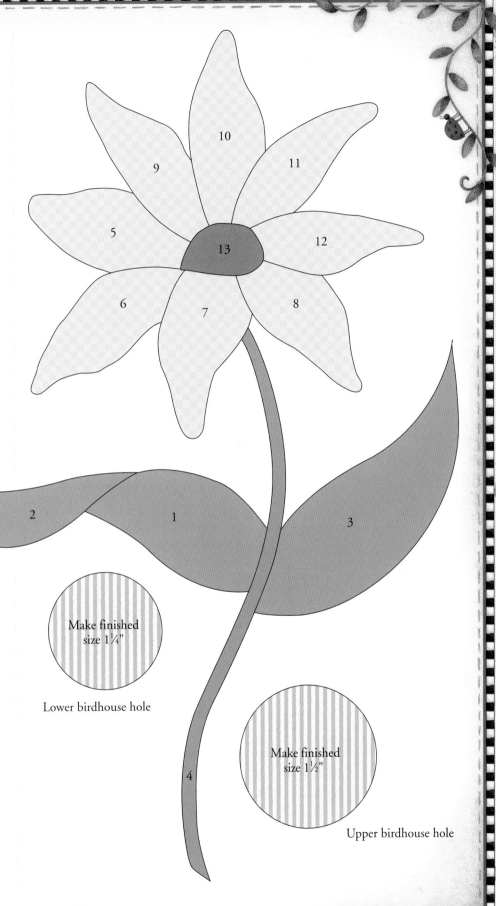

Make finished size 1¼"

Lower birdhouse hole

Make finished size 1½"

Upper birdhouse hole

Lots of Ladybugs Quilt

Remember that favorite childhood chant—
"Ladybug, ladybug fly away home?"
It seems the ladybugs have come to
light on the summer-green leaves of
this delightful quilt.

Lots of Ladybugs Quilt
Finished Quilt Size: 54" x 78" (not including prairie points)
Photo: page 53

Black buttons and
a touch of appliqué add whimsical
charm to the quick-pieced blocks, and
prairie point frame. Read all
instructions before beginning and
use ¼"-wide seams throughout.

FABRIC REQUIREMENTS

Fabric A (Leaves and Stems) - ¾ yard
each of four different green fabrics

Fabric B (Ladybug Bodies) - ⅓ yard
each of four different red fabrics

Fabric C (Ladybug Heads) - Assorted
black scraps

Fabric D (Background) - 2½ yards

Accent Border - ⅓ yard

Outside Border - ⅝ yard

Prairie Points - 1⅛ yards

Backing - 3½ yards

Lightweight Batting - 58" x 82" piece

192 assorted black buttons (⅜" - ¾")

CUTTING THE STRIPS AND PIECES

Read first paragraph of Cutting the Strips and Pieces on page 7.

	FIRST CUT		SECOND CUT	
	Number of Strips or Pieces	Dimensions	Number of Pieces	Dimensions
FABRIC A Repeat for each of four fabrics	4	4½" x 42"	30	4½" squares (leaves)
	2	2½" x 42"	24	2½" squares (leaves)
	1	1½" x 42"	12	1½" squares (leaves)
	1	1" x 42"	6	1" x 7" (stems)
FABRIC B Repeat for each of four fabrics	2	4½" x 42"	12	4½" squares
FABRIC C	48	1½" squares		
FABRIC D	18	4½" x 42"	144	4½" squares
ACCENT BORDER	7	1½" x 42"		
OUTSIDE BORDER	7	2½" x 42"		
PRAIRIE POINTS	9	4" x 42"	84	4" squares

MAKING THE BLOCKS

You will be making 24 leaf blocks. Each leaf block includes 2 ladybugs. The leaf block finishes 12" square. The "ladybug in the leaf" finishes 4" square.

Whenever possible, use the Assembly Line Method on page 110. Press in direction of arrows.

Ladybug Blocks

1. Refer to Quick Corner Triangle directions on page 110. For each block, sew two matching 2½" Fabric A squares to each 4½" Fabric B square. Press. Make forty-eight total.

Repeat to sew a matching 1½" Fabric A square and a scrappy 1½" Fabric C square to remaining two corners of each step 1 unit. Press.

B = 4½ x 4½
A = 2½ x 2½
Make 48

C = 1½ x 1½
A = 1½ x 1½

Leaf Blocks

1. Refer to Hand Appliqué directions on page 110. Hand or machine appliqué one 1" x 7" Fabric A piece diagonally over a 4½" Fabric D square as shown. Make twenty-four.

4½
4½

Make 24

2. Refer to Quick Corner Triangle directions on page 110. Sew 4½" Fabric A and Fabric D squares to make ninety-six units. Press.

A = 4½ x 4½
D = 4½ x 4½
Make 96

3. Sew unit from step 2, a matching-color 4½" Fabric A square and a matching color appliquéd Fabric D square from step 1 in a row as shown. Press. Make twenty-four.

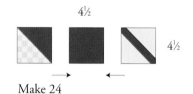

4½
4½

Make 24

4. Sew two matching ladybug blocks and a matching-color unit from step 2 in a row as shown. Press. Make twenty-four.

Make 24

5. Sew a remaining 4½" Fabric B square and two matching units from step 2 in a row as shown. Press. Make twenty-four.

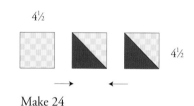

4½
4½

Make 24

6. Arrange matching-color rows from steps 3, 4, and 5 as shown. Sew the rows. Press.

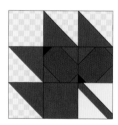

Make 24

ASSEMBLY

1. Refer to project layout on page 50 and color photo on page 53. Arrange blocks in a pleasing arrangement of six horizontal rows of four blocks each, rotating blocks as shown. Sew blocks into rows. Press seams in opposite directions from row to row.

2. Sew rows together. Press.

BORDERS

1. Cut one 1½" x 42" accent border strip in half and sew halves to two 1½" x 42" strips. Sew remaining 1½" x 42" accent border strips together in pairs. Repeat for outside border.

2. Sew 1½" accent borders to 2½" outside borders lengthwise. Press toward outside border.

3. Measure quilt through center vertically and horizontally.

4. Fold each border unit crosswise to find its midpoint and mark with a pin. Using quilt dimensions measured in step 3, measure each border unit from its midpoint and pin-mark border ends to show where edges of quilt will be.

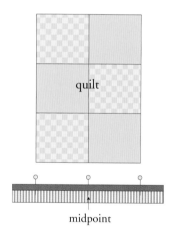

quilt

midpoint

7. Sew border to quilt, stopping and starting with a backstitch ¼" from pinmarked end points. Do not sew past pin marks at either end. Repeat to sew all four border units to quilt.

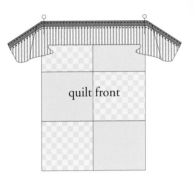

8. Fold one corner diagonally, right sides together, matching and pinning marked diagonal sewing lines. End points of adjacent seams should match.

Begin sewing with a backstitch at point where side seams ended. Sew to end of marked line at outside edge of strip. Trim excess border ¼" from seam and press open. Repeat on remaining corners. Press border seams to outside and mitered seams open.

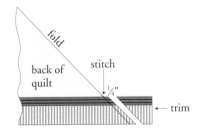

5. Beginning at a marked end point, draw a 45 degree diagonal line to represent mitered seam line. Repeat on opposite end of strip, drawing a mirror image diagonal line. Repeat for all four border units.

6. Align a border unit to quilt with accent border closest to quilt center. Pin at midpoints and pin-marked ends first, and then along entire side easing to fit if necessary.

LAYERING AND FINISHING

1. Use 4" squares to make 84 Prairie Points, folding each twice along the diagonal as shown.

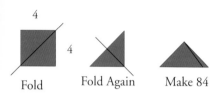

Fold   Fold Again   Make 84

2. Starting at the center and working outwards, align and pin raw edges of 17 Prairie Points along top edge of quilt as shown, nesting one inside folds of another if necessary to adjust total width. Repeat on bottom edge of quilt.

Quilt Top

3. Pin 25 Prairie Points to each side of quilt in the same way. Triangle edges should meet at quilt corners.

4. Sew all Prairie Points to quilt with ¼" seams. Do not fold outwards.

5. Cut backing crosswise into two equal pieces. Sew together to make one 63" x 84" (approximate) backing piece. Arrange and baste backing, batting, and top together referring to Layering the Quilt directions on page 111.

6. Machine or hand quilt as desired, carefully avoiding prairie points. Leave 1" from all edges free from quilting.

7. Trim batting and backing to match quilt top, then trim an additional ¼" of batting from all sides.

8. Fold Prairie Points away from quilt, pointing them outward and seams under quilt top. Press. Turn under ¼" of backing and hand stitch in place, covering seams. Add more quilting around edges if desired.

9. Refer to layout on page 50 and color photo on page 53. Sew four small black buttons to each ladybug body as shown. (You may wish to vary the number of "spots").

Little Ladybug Wallhanging

Here's a smaller version of the Lots of Ladybugs Quilt pictured on page 53. What a perfect way to celebrate the arrival of summer! Read all instructions before beginning and use ¼" seam allowances throughout. Finished size will be 30" square. (not including prairie points)

FABRIC REQUIREMENTS

Fabric A - (⅝ yard) or scraps
   Twenty 4½" squares (leaves)
   Sixteen 2½" squares (leaves)
   Eight 1½" squares (leaves)
   Four 1" x 7" strips (stems)

Fabric B (Ladybug Bodies) - scraps
   Eight 4½" squares

Fabric C (Ladybug Heads) - scraps
   Eight 1½" squares

Fabric D (Background) - ½ yard
   Three 4½" x 42" strips, cut into
     Twenty-four 4½" squares

Accent Border - ¼ yard
   Two 1½" x 24½" strips
   Two 1½" x 26½" strips

Outside Border - ⅓ yard
   Two 2½" x 26½" strips
   Two 2½" x 30½" strips

Prairie Points - ½ yard
   Four 4" x 42" strips, cut into
     Thirty-two 4" squares

Backing - 1 yard

Lightweight batting - 33" x 33" piece

Small Buttons - 32

MAKING THE BLOCKS

Refer to instructions in Lots of Ladybugs Quilt to make four leaf blocks. Each leaf block includes two ladybugs. The leaf block finishes 12" square. Stitch the four leaf blocks together and add borders.

BORDERS

1. Sew 1½" x 24½" accent border strips to top and bottom. Press toward border strips.

2. Sew 1½" x 26½" accent border strips to sides. Press.

3. Sew 2½" x 26½" outside border strips to top and bottom. Press.

4. Sew 2½" x 30½" outside border strips to sides. Press.

LAYERING AND FINISHING

1. Refer to Lots of Ladybugs Quilt and use 4" squares to make thirty-two Prairie Points.

Ladybug House

Ladybug House

Our feathered friends *will fly away home to this loveable birdhouse. A whimsical ladybug welcomes them to this easy-to-paint haven.*

Crackle medium *and antiquing glaze give this painted project a vintage look. The same process can be used on flowerpots or furniture. You can have ladybugs everywhere!*

MATERIALS NEEDED

Small, unpainted birdhouse
Acrylic craft paint: country red, ivory,
   black, and green for house
   and ladybug
Assorted paint brushes
Ruler

Two-step crackle medium
Tracing paper
Graphite transfer paper
Scotch Magic™ Tape
Matte spray varnish
Antiquing medium

PAINTING THE HOUSE

Refer to the color photo for guidance as needed.

1. Paint roof with two coats of country red acrylic paint. Allow to dry thoroughly.

2. Paint roof with ½" random black polka dots.

3. Paint roof edge ivory. Measure and use ruler to mark ¼" checks on ivory edge. Paint every other check with black paint.

4. Paint house ivory with two or three coats, until well covered.

5. Following manufacturer's directions for crackle medium, apply thick coat of part one to the walls of the house. Allow to dry thoroughly. Apply part two of crackle medium. Cracks are clear until house is antiqued.

6. Paint base of house and roof decoration with two coats of green paint. (On the sample shown, the roof decoration is a piece of dowel along the top edge of the roof.)

7. Trace ladybug pattern below onto tracing paper. Position tracing paper on birdhouse front where you wish ladybug to appear. Tape in place, leaving one side open. Slide graphite paper under tracing paper, and use ballpoint pen to transfer design. Remove tape, tracing, and graphite paper.

8. Refer to color photo and paint ladybug in colors of choice. Allow to dry thoroughly.

9. Apply a coat of matte spray varnish, and follow manufacturer's instructions to apply antiquing medium to entire house. Finish with final coat of matte spray varnish.

Ladybug pattern

Summer ~ *Ladybug House*

Garden Stepping Stone

On a warm *summer day take a stroll down the garden path highlighted with the beauty of your flowers and the elegance of this glass mosaic stepping stone.*

Don't stop with *this project. Use other appliqués in this book to create mosaic birdhouse flowerpots, a birdhouse birdbath, or a garden bench. The possibilities are endless.*

Garden Stepping Stone

MATERIALS NEEDED

Fine-point felt-tip pen
Clear self-adhesive vinyl - 18" x 18"
16" square concrete stepping stone
Assorted colors scrap glass
Ceramic tile adhesive
Tilers grout *
Sealant
Rags/sponge/wooden skewer stick
Safety glasses

*If less than ¼" space between glass
  use non-sanded grout, larger spaces
  between glass use a sanded grout.

58

PREPARING THE STEPPING STONE

1. Following diagram below, draw birdhouse design on the clear non-stick side of the self-adhesive vinyl. (DO NOT DRAW ON PAPER SIDE)

2. Peel backing off of vinyl. Fold under outside edges approximately ½" to itself to form a non-stick edge.

3. Wearing safety glasses and using glass mosaic cutting pliers, break glass into irregular shapes.

4. Place glass right side down onto sticky side of vinyl in a pleasing pattern.

5. Leave a minimum of ⅟₁₆" to ⅛" space between each piece of glass.

MAKING BIRDHOUSE STEPPING STONE

1. Apply ceramic tile adhesive to the clean surface of 16" concrete stone.

2. Carefully lift the vinyl with glass adhering to it, and place glass onto adhesive area.

3. Slowly peel away vinyl leaving glass on tile adhesive. Clean excess adhesive between glass with stick.

4. Let adhesive dry a minimum of 24 hours.

5. Following manufacturer's instructions, mix, and apply finish grout.

6. Apply sealant following product directions.

Mosaic Ideas

Decorate terra cotta pots and planters with the small birdhouse appliqués found in the Garden Tool Caddy section.

Decorate wooden frames.

Broken dishes? Don't despair; use in place of colored glass to create a mosaic piece.

Continue your outside theme by making mosaic pieces for the inside of your home.

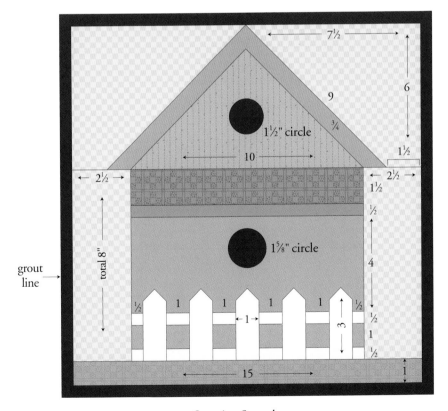

Stepping Stone layout

Garden Tool Caddy

Garden Tool Caddy

A purchased *organizer, personalized with your choice of quick-fuse appliqués, makes the perfect catch-all for gardening gloves, tools, and seed packets.*

Read all instructions before beginning, and use ¼"-wide seams throughout.

MATERIALS AND FABRIC NEEDED

Pocket bucket organizer - Comes in various colors and various pocket layouts.

Assorted scraps to coordinate with organizer colors for birdhouse appliqués

Accent Trim - See Assembly directions on page 61.

Binding - See Assembly directions on page 61.

Heavy duty fusible web - ⅛ yard

Bucket

ASSEMBLY

1. Remove purchased binding from organizer. Set it aside for now.

2. Measure width of organizer from raw edge to raw edge along its top edge. Cut one 2¼"-wide strip to that measurement from the accent trim fabric.

3. Turn under ¼"-wide seam allowance along long raw edges of 2¼"-wide accent trim strip, and press. Pin strip along top edge of organizer and topstitch in place by hand or machine.

Bucket

4. Refer to Quick-Fuse Appliqué directions on page 111. Trace one birdhouse appliqué design for each organizer pocket from patterns below. Center and quick-fuse designs to pockets, referring to color photo for placement.

5. Measure length of binding removed from organizer in step 1. Cut 2¾"-wide strips to equal that measurement, plus a little extra for seams and finishing. Attach binding, referring to Binding the Quilt directions on page 111.

Tool Caddy
Appliqués

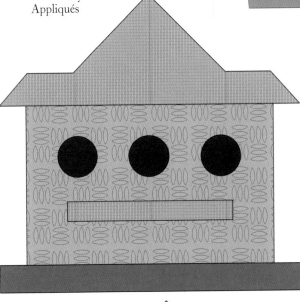

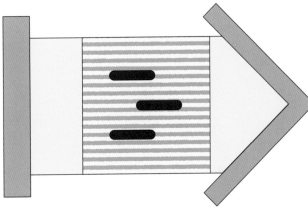

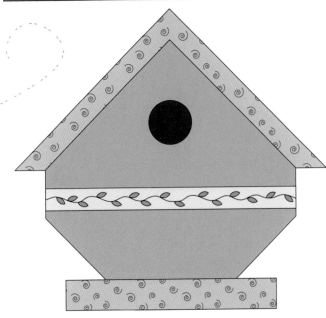

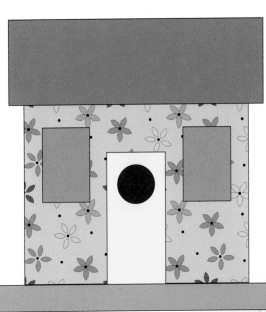

Autumn

It sneaks up on us every year. The leaves of gold and red begin to drift to the ground, and the harvest pumpkins are almost ripe on the vines. There's just a little chill in the afternoon air, and we know, once again, that glorious autumn has arrived.

Surrounded by the rich, vibrant colors of the season, the children head back to school, and our faithful friends begin to feather their nests or to think of their journeys south to find warmer homes. It's a great time to add cozy touches to your nest, too, with warm and wonderful projects created to celebrate the golden glow of autumn.

Fall Flight Quilt

You'll welcome those first cool autumn nights as you snuggle under this cozy quilt! We've chosen a variety of warm browns for our soaring birds, winging south over a crisp blue sky.

Two-color sashing creates a charming effect, and snappy four-patch corner squares add pizzazz. Read all instructions before beginning and use ¼" seams throughout.

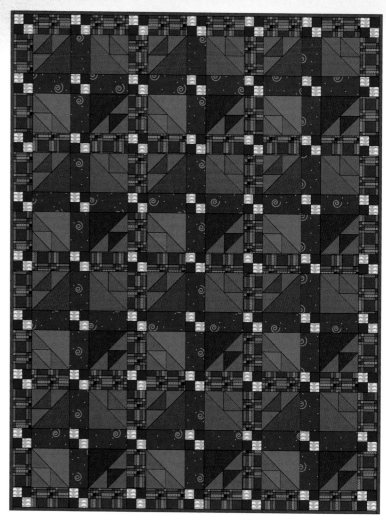

Fall Flight Quilt
Finished Size: 58" x 76"
Photo: page 67

FABRIC REQUIREMENTS

Fabric A (Birds) - ¼ yard *each* of eight different brown fabrics or fat quarters (18" x 22")

Fabric B (Background) - 1⅛ yards

Fabric C and D (Four Patches) ½ yard *each* of two contrasting fabrics

Inside Sashing - ⅞ yard

Outside Sashing - 1⅙ yards

Binding - ⅝ yard

Backing - 3⅝ yards

Lightweight Batting - 62" x 80"

CUTTING THE STRIPS AND PIECES

Read first paragraph of Cutting the Strips and Pieces on page 7.

	FIRST CUT		SECOND CUT	
	Number of Strips	Dimensions	Number of Pieces	Dimensions
FABRIC A Repeat for each of eight fabrics	1 1	6⅞" x 22" 3½" x 22"	3 6	6⅞" squares 3½" squares
FABRIC B	4 3	3½" x 42" 3⅞" x 42"	48 48	3½" squares 3⅞" squares
FABRIC C AND D Repeat for each fabric	7	2" x 42"		
INSIDE SASHING	8	3½" x 42"	48	3½" x 6½"
OUTSIDE SASHING	11	3½" x 42"	62	3½" x 6½"
BINDING	7	2¾" x 42"		

MAKING THE BLOCKS

You will be making forty-eight "bird" blocks and sixty-three four-patch corner squares. Whenever possible, use the Assembly Line Method on page 110. Press in direction of arrows in diagrams.

Bird Blocks

1. Refer to Quick Corner Triangle directions on page 110. Using 3½" Fabric A and Fabric B squares, make forty-eight units. Press.

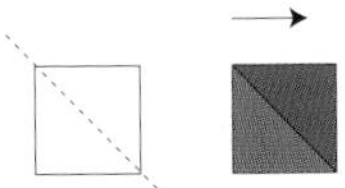

A = 3½ x 3½
B = 3½ x 3½
Make 48

2. Cut 3⅞" Fabric B squares in half once diagonally to make ninety-six triangles. Sew triangles to adjacent sides of each unit from step 1. Press.

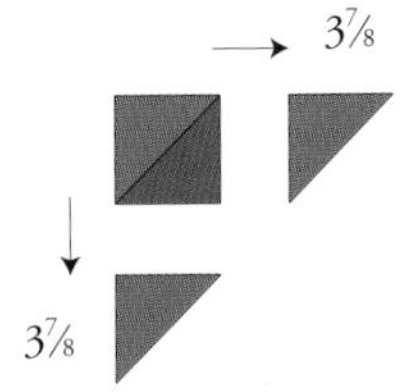

Make 48

3. Cut each 6⅞" Fabric A triangle in half once diagonally to make forty-eight triangles. Sew each triangle to a matching-color unit from step 2 as shown. Press. Block measures 6½" x 6½".

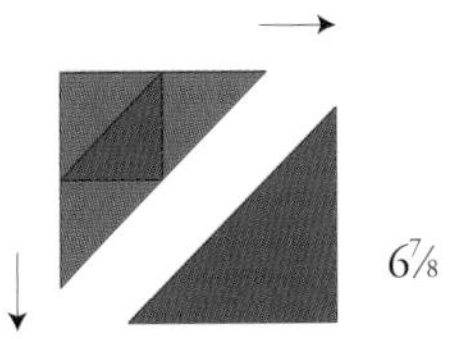

Make 48

Four-Patch Corner Squares

1. Sew 2" x 42" Fabric C and Fabric D strips together in pairs to make seven identical strip sets. Press toward darker fabric. Cut one hundred twenty-six 2" segments.

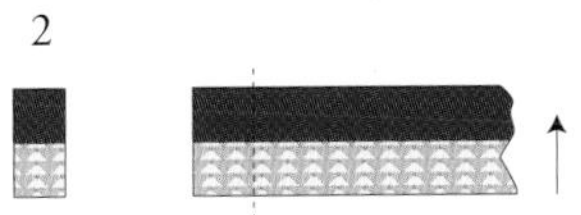

Cut 126 — Make 7 strip sets

2. Sew segments from step 1 together in pairs. Press. Make sixty-three.

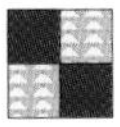

Make 63

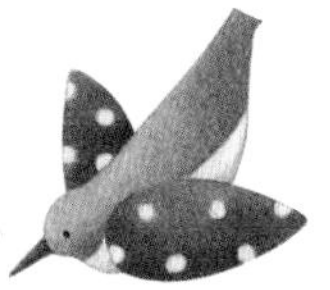

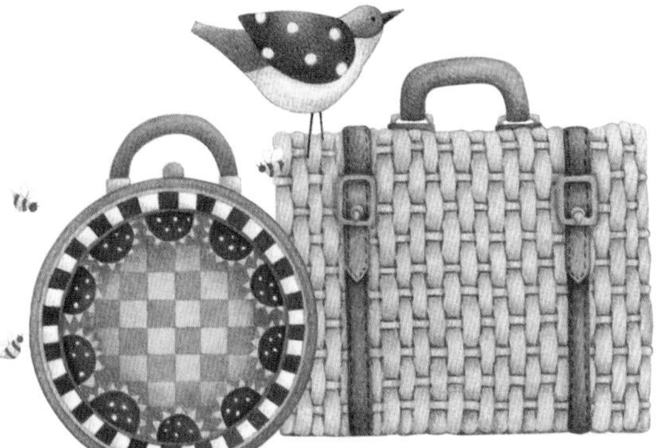

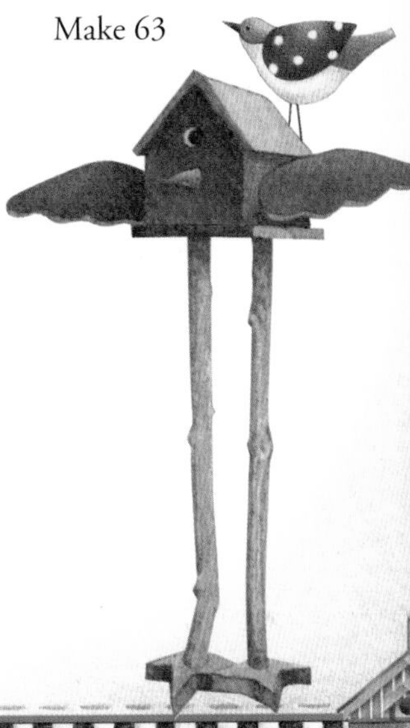

ASSEMBLY

1. Lay out six bird blocks, three 3½" x 6½" inside sashing pieces, and four 3½" x 6½" outside sashing pieces to make a horizontal row as shown. Sew blocks and strips together. Press seams toward sashing strips. Make eight rows.

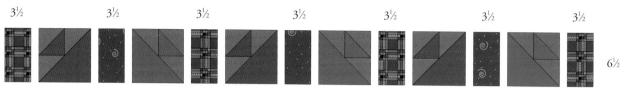

Make 8 Rows

2. Alternate seven pieced corner squares and six 6½" x 3½" outside sashing pieces to make a horizontal row as shown. Sew squares and strips together. Press seams toward sashing strips. Make five rows.

Make 5 Rows

3. Repeat step 2, substituting the 6½" x 3½" inside sashing strips for the outside sashing strips. Make four rows.

Make 4 Rows

4. Referring to layout on page 64 and color photo, lay out rows from steps 1 through 3 as shown. Join rows and press.

LAYERING AND FINISHING

1. Cut backing fabric crosswise into two equal pieces. Sew pieces together to make one 65" x 84" (approximate) backing piece. Arrange and baste backing, batting, and top together, referring to Layering the Quilt directions on page 111.

2. Machine or hand quilt as desired.

3. Cut one 2 ¾" x 42" binding strip in half and sew halves to two 2 ¾" x 42" strips. Sew remaining 2 ¾" x 42" binding strips in pairs. Using shorter strips for top and bottom and longer strips for sides, refer to Binding the Quilt directions on page 111 to finish.

Back -to- School Birdhouse

No matter how *grown up we get, we never seem to forget the excitement of back-to-school days. Revisit those wonderful times while stitching on this nostalgic schoolhouse.*

A log-cabin *printed fabric adds interest to the border without taking a lot of time. Read all instructions before beginning and use ¼"-wide seam allowances throughout.*

Back to School Birdhouse
Finished Quilt Size: 37" x 41"
Photo: page 72

FABRIC REQUIREMENTS

Fabric A (Small Gable) - Scraps
Fabric B (Large Gable) - ⅛ yard*
Fabric C (Schoolhouse Trim) - ⅛ yard
Fabric D (Schoolhouse and Pencil
    Background, Inside and Middle
    Borders) - ⅔ yard
Fabric E (Roof Appliqués and
    Birdhouse Hole) - ⅛ yard
Fabric F (Windows) - Scraps
Fabric G (Schoolhouse Front)
    ⅙ yard*
Fabric H (Lower Wall) - Scraps
Fabric I (Door and Shutters) - Scraps
Fabric J (Grass) - ⅛ yard
Fabric K (Steps) - Scraps
Fabric L (Pencils) - ⅙ yard

Fabric M (Pencil Points) - Scraps
Fabric N (Erasers) - Scraps
Fabric O (Apples) - ¼ yard (total)
    assorted red scraps**
Fabric P (Background and Sashing
    for Apple Blocks) - ½ yard
Fabric Q (Leaves) - Scraps
Fabric R (Apple Stems) - Scraps
Outside Border - ½ yard
Binding - ⅜ yard
Backing - 1⅙ yards
Lightweight Batting - 41" x 45" piece
    * We used ¼ yard (total) of the same
    fabric for the large gable and
    schoolhouse front. (Fabric G)
    ** We used five different red fabrics.

CUTTING THE STRIPS AND PIECES

Read first paragraph of Cutting the Strips and Pieces on page 7.

	FIRST CUT		SECOND CUT	
	Number of Strips or Pieces	Dimensions	Number of Pieces	Dimensions
FABRIC A	1	4½" x 3½"		
FABRIC B	1	3½" x 42"	2	3½" x 5½"
			1	3½" x 14½"
			2	2½" squares
FABRIC C	1	1½" x 14½"		
FABRIC D	2	7½" squares		
	5	1½" x 42"	2	1½" x 7½"
			16	1½" squares
			2	1½" x 16½"
			2	1½" x 20½"
			2	1½" x 24½"
	1	2½" x 42"	2	2½" x 7½"
			4	2½" squares
FABRIC E	1	1½" x 42"	2	1½" x 12"
			2	1" x 4"
			1	2¼" square
FABRIC F	2	2½" x 4"		
FABRIC G	1	1½" x 42"	4	1½" x 2½"
	1	1¾" x 42"	4	1¾" x 6"
	1	2" x 3½"		
FABRIC H	2	5" x 2"		
FABRIC I	1	3½" x 6" (door)		
	4	1" x 4" (shutters)		
FABRIC J	1	1½" x 42"	2	1½" x 7"
			2	1½" x 6½"
FABRIC K	1	1½" x 3½"		
	1	1½" x 4½"		
FABRIC L	2	2½" x 42"	4	2½" x 6½"
			4	2½" x 7½"
FABRIC M	1	1½" x 42"	8	1½" x 2½"
FABRIC N	4	2½" squares		
FABRIC O	20	3½" squares		
FABRIC P	6	1½" x 42"	120	1½" squares
			8	1½" x 3½"
	1	4½" x 42"	2	4½" x 6½"
			2	4½" x 3½"
			8	4½" x 1½"
FABRIC Q	20	1½" squares		
FABRIC R	20	1½" squares		

MAKING THE BLOCKS

In addition to the center schoolhouse block, you will be making eight pencils (four each in two different sizes) and twenty apple blocks. Whenever possible, use the Assembly Line Method, page 110. Press in direction of arrows.

Schoolhouse Block

1. Refer to Quick Corner Triangle directions on page 110. Sew 2½" Fabric B squares to 4½" x 3½" Fabric A piece as shown. Press.

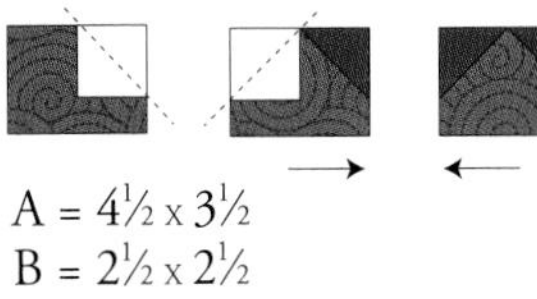

A = 4½ x 3½
B = 2½ x 2½

2. Sew unit from step 1 between two 3½" x 5½" Fabric B pieces. Press.

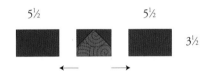

5½   5½   3½

3. Sew unit from step 2 between 3½" x 14½" Fabric B strip and 1½" x 14½" Fabric C strip. Press.

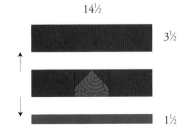

14½   3½   1½

4. Refer to Quick Corner Triangle directions on page 110. Sew two 7½" Fabric D squares to unit from step 3 as shown. Press.

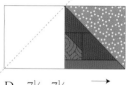

D = 7½ x 7½

D = 7½ x 7½

14½

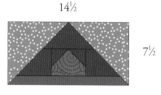

7½

5. Sew unit from step 4 between two 1½" x 7½" Fabric D pieces. Press.

6. Sew 1½" x 2½" Fabric G pieces to each 2½" x 4" Fabric F piece as shown. Press. Make two.

2½

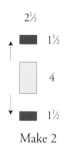

1½

4

1½

Make 2

7. Sew each unit from step 6 between two 1¾" x 6" Fabric G pieces. Press. Make two.

1¾   2½   1¾

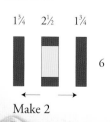

6

Make 2

8. Sew one 5" x 2" Fabric H piece to each unit from step 7 as shown. Press. Make two.

5

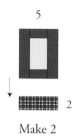

2

Make 2

9. Sew 2" x 3½" Fabric G piece to 3½" x 6" Fabric I piece as shown. Press.

3½

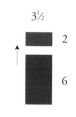

2

6

10. Arrange and sew two 2½" x 7½" Fabric D pieces, two units from step 8, and unit from step 9 as shown. Press.

2½   2½

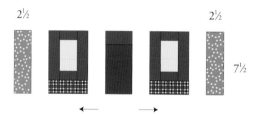

7½

11. Sew 1½" x 3½" Fabric K piece between two 1½" x 7" Fabric J pieces. Label this Row A, and press. Repeat to sew 1½" x 4½" Fabric K piece between two 1½" x 6½" Fabric J pieces. Label this Row B, and press.

7   3½   7
Row A   1½

6½   4½   6½
Row B   1½

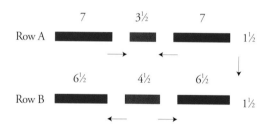

12. Refer to layout on page 68 and color photo on page 72. Arrange and sew unit from step 5, unit from step 10, and rows A and B from step 11 as shown. Press. Block will measure 16½".

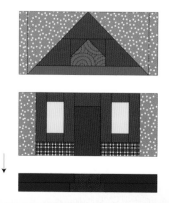

16½

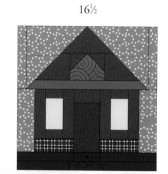

16½

MAKING AND ADDING PENCIL BLOCKS

1. Refer to Quick Corner Triangle directions on page 110. Sew two 1½" Fabric D squares to each 1½" x 2½" Fabric M piece as shown. Press. Make eight.

D = 1½ x 1½
M = 1½ x 2½
Make 8

2. Arrange and sew two units from step 1, one 2½" Fabric D square, and two 2½" x 6½" Fabric L pieces as shown. Press. Make two.

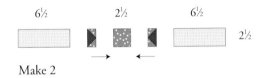

Make 2

3. Sew one 1½" x 16½" Fabric D strip to each unit from step 2. Press seams toward strip. Make two.

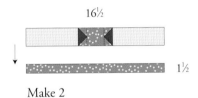

Make 2

4. Refer to layout on page 68 and color photo on page 72. Sew one unit from step 3 to top and bottom of schoolhouse block, positioning Fabric D strip closest to center block. Press seams toward strip.

5. Sew two remaining units from step 1, one 2½" Fabric D square, two 2½" x 7½" Fabric L pieces, and two 2½" Fabric N squares as shown. Press. Make two.

Make 2

6. Sew units from step 5 to sides of quilt. Press seams toward center block.

7. Sew 1½" x 20½" Fabric D inside border strips to top and bottom of quilt. Press seams toward border strips. Sew 1½" x 24½" inside border strips to sides. Press.

8. Trace appliqué design from page 37. Make template and cut one birdhouse hole #1 from Fabric E, adding ¼" seam allowance. Machine stitch or refer to Hand Appliqué on page 110. Appliqué two 1½" x 12" Fabric E roof pieces over large gable and two 1" x 4" Fabric E roof pieces over small gable. Follow seam lines, extending and squaring ends as shown. Appliqué one 1" x 4" Fabric I shutter piece on opposite sides of each window, and the birdhouse hole on the small gable.

MAKING AND ADDING APPLE BLOCKS

1. Refer to Quick Corner Triangle directions on page 110. Sew a 1½" Fabric P square to each corner of a 3½" Fabric O square. Press. Make twenty.

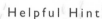

O = 3½ x 3½
P = 1½ x 1½
Make 20

2. Sew 1½" Fabric P and 1½" Fabric Q squares together in pairs, referring to Quick Corner Triangle directions on page 110. Press. Make twenty.

P = 1½ x 1½
Q = 1½ x 1½
Make 20

3. Sew 1½" Fabric P square, 1½" Fabric R square, and one unit from step 2 to make a row. Press. Make twenty rows.

1½   1½   1½

Make 20

4. Sew units from step 1 to rows from step 3 as shown. Press. Block will measure 3½" x 4½".

Helpful Hint

After cutting strips and pieces place them in labeled zip lock bags. It will make organization easier and speed the piecing process.

5. Lay out four 4½" x 1½" Fabric P sashing pieces, four apple blocks, and one 4½" x 6½" Fabric P piece to make a horizontal row as shown. Sew blocks and strips together. Press. Make two rows.

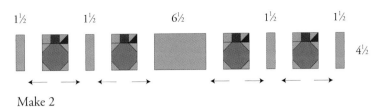

Make 2

6. Lay out six apple blocks, four 1½" x 3½" Fabric P sashing pieces, and one 4½" x 3½" Fabric P piece to make a vertical row as shown. Sew blocks and strips together. Press. Make two rows.

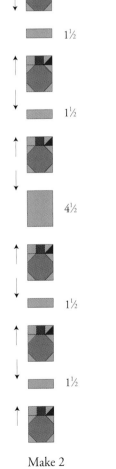

Make 2

7. Referring to layout on page 68 and color photo, sew units from step 5 to top and bottom of quilt. Press toward quilt center. Sew units from step 6 to sides. Press.

BORDERS

		Number of Strips	Dimensions
	MIDDLE BORDER	4	1½" x 42
	OUTSIDE BORDER	4	3½" x 42"
	BINDING	4	2¾" x 42"

1. Measure quilt through center from side to side. Trim two 1½" x 42" Fabric D middle border strips to this measurement. Sew to top and bottom. Press seams toward middle border.

2. Measure quilt through center from top to bottom, including border. Trim remaining 1½" x 42" Fabric D middle border strips to this measurement. Sew to sides. Press.

3. Repeat steps 1 and 2 to fit, trim, and sew 3½" x 42" outside border strips to top, bottom, and sides of quilt. Press seams toward outside border.

LAYERING AND FINISHING

1. Arrange and baste backing, batting, and top together, referring to Layering the Quilt directions on page 111.

2. Machine or hand quilt as desired.

3. Using the four 2¾" x 42" binding strips, refer to Binding the Quilt directions on page 111 to finish.

Apple Harvest

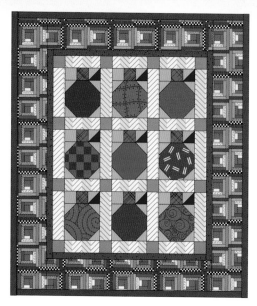

Whether you prefer *them red or green, sweet or tart, you'll find the apples in this yummy wallhanging hard to resist!*

Hang it in *your entry hall, country kitchen, or breakfast room to bring a touch of autumn's bounty indoors to enjoy. Read all instructions before beginning and use ¼" seams throughout.*

Apple Harvest
Finished Size: 20" x 23"
Photo: page 76

FABRIC REQUIREMENTS

Fabric A (Apples) - ⅛ yard or
    assorted scraps*
Fabric B (Background) - ⅛ yard
Fabric C (Stems) - Scraps
Fabric D (Leaves) - Scraps
Sashing - ⅙ yard
Corner Squares - ⅛ yard
Accent Border - ⅛ yard
Outside Border - ¼ yard

Binding - ⅜ yard
Backing - ¾ yard
Lightweight Batting - 24" x 27"
* We used one green and eight red
    fabrics.

CUTTING THE STRIPS AND PIECES

Read first paragraph of Cutting the Strips and Pieces on page 7.

		FIRST CUT		SECOND CUT	
		Number of Strips or Pieces	Dimensions	Number of Pieces	Dimensions
	FABRIC A	9	3½" squares		
	FABRIC B	2	1½" x 42"	54	1½" squares
	FABRIC C	9	1½" squares		
	FABRIC D	9	1½" squares		
	SASHING	3	1½" x 42"	12	1½" x 3½"
				12	1½" x 4½"
	CORNER SQUARES	1	1½" x 42"	16	1½" squares
	ACCENT BORDER	2	1" x 42"	2	1" x 13½"
				2	1" x 17½"
	OUTSIDE BORDER	2	3" x 42"	2	3" x 14½"
				2	3" x 22½"
	BINDING	3	2¾" x 42"		

MAKING THE APPLE BLOCKS

You will be making 9 apple blocks. Whenever possible, use the Asembly Line Method on page 110. Press in direction of arrows.

1. Refer to Quick Corner Triangle directions on page 110. Sew a 1½" Fabric B square to each corner of a 3½" Fabric A square. Press. Make nine.

A = 3½ x 3½
B = 1½ x 1½
Make 9

2. Sew 1½" Fabric B and 1½" Fabric D squares together in pairs, referring to Quick Corner Triangle directions on page 110. Press. Make nine.

B = 1½ x 1½
D = 1½ x 1½
Make 9

3. Sew a remaining 1½" Fabric B square, a 1½" Fabric C square, and one unit from step 2 to make a row. Press. Make nine rows.

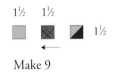

1½   1½

                    1½

Make 9

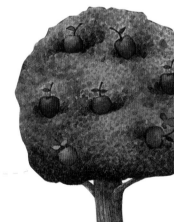

4. Sew a unit from step 1 to a row from step 3 as shown. Press. Make nine.

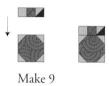

Make 9

ASSEMBLY

1. Lay out four 1½" x 4½" sashing strips and three apple blocks, alternating them to make a horizontal row as shown. Sew blocks and strips together. Press toward sashing. Make three rows, placing the green apple block in the center of one row.

1½   1½   1½   1½

4½

Make 3

2. Alternate four 1½" corner squares and three 1½" x 3½" sashing pieces to make a horizontal row as shown. Sew squares and strips together. Press toward sashing. Make four rows.

1½   3½   1½   3½   1½   3½   1½

1½

Make 4

3. Referring to layout on page 74 and color photo below, arrange rows from steps 1 and 2 as shown. Join rows and press.

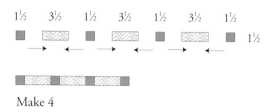

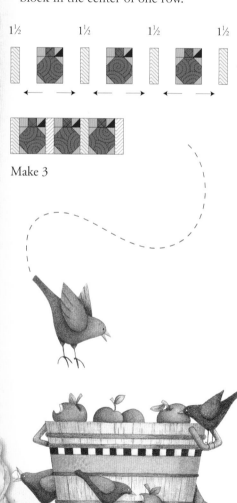

BORDERS

Sew short accent borders to top and bottom of quilt. Press seams toward accent border. Sew long accent border strips to sides. Press. Repeat to add outside border strips to top, bottom, and sides. Press.

LAYERING AND FINISHING

1. Arrange and baste backing, batting, and top together, referring to Layering the Quilt directions on page 111.

2. Machine or hand quilt as desired.

3. Cut one 2¾" x 42" binding strip in half. Using shorter strips for top and bottom and longer strips for sides, refer to Binding the Quilt directions on page 111 to finish.

Class Act Wallhanging

Use photo transfer and a few quick construction changes to transform the "Apple Harvest" wall quilt into a wallhanging to give to a special teacher or administrator. You could use a snapshot of a class group, an old school house, or a delightful piece of artwork drawn by a child. Finished size will be 20" x 30".

CUTTING THE STRIPS AND PIECES

Fabric A - Six 3½" squares

Fabric B - Thirty-six 1½" squares

Fabric C - Six 1½" squares

Fabric D - Six 1½" squares

Fabric E (first photo border)
    Two 1" x 10½" pieces
    Two 1" x 9½" pieces

Fabric F (second photo border)
    Four 1½" x 11½" pieces

Sashing - Twelve 1½" x 3½" pieces
    Eight 1½" x 4½" pieces

Corner Squares - Sixteen 1½" squares

Accent Border - Two 1" x 13½" strips
    Two 1" x 24½" strips

Outside Border - Two 3" x 14½" strips
    Two 3" x 29½" strips

Photo transfer fabric - 12" x 14" piece

Binding - Three 2¾" x 42" strips

8" x 10" photo* or drawing

*Obtain photographer's permission if using professional photos

ASSEMBLY AND FINISHING

1. Photocopy a color or black and white image on image transfer paper following manufacturer's directions. Center and press on a 12" x 14" piece of fabric. A copy shop or scrapbook store may be able to make a better quality transfer for you. After transferring the image to fabric, trim the fabric to 10½" x 8½".

2. Sew the fabric photo between two 1" x 10½" Fabric E pieces. Press toward Fabric E. Sew two 1" x 9½" pieces to sides of fabric photo.

3. Repeat step 2 adding Fabric F pieces to top, bottom, and sides.

4. Follow instructions on page 75 and 76 to make six apple blocks. Follow instructions on page 76 to add sashing to apple blocks.

5. Sew unit from step 3 between apple block rows.

6. Continue following instructions on page 77 for Borders and Layering and Finishing using the sizes indicated for "Class Act" accent and outside borders.

Falling Leaves
Table Runner & Placemats

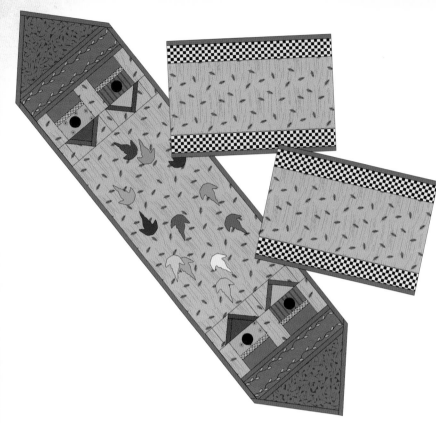

Falling Leaves Table Runner & Placemats
Finished Table Runner Size: 14" x 59"
Finished Placemat Size: 19" x 13"
Photo: page 81

A sprinkling of *leaves in rich, earthy colors dance merrily across our charming table runner, signaling that autumn is near. Scrappy birdhouses and a whimsical print form the picture perfect frame.*

Why not whip *up a batch of our oh-so-easy autumn placemats to match? Read all instructions before beginning and use ¼"-wide seams throughout.*

FABRIC REQUIREMENTS

Table Runner:

Birdhouses - Assorted scraps in a variety of colors

Fabric A (Background) - ⅝ yard

Fabric B (Trim) - ⅛ yard

Fabric C (Border) - ⅛ yard

Fabric D (Points) - ⅓ yard

Leaf Appliqués - Assorted scraps in a variety of colors

Binding - ⅜ yard *

Backing - ⅞ yard

Lightweight Batting - 18" x 62" piece

* May substitute 4 yards of doublefold bias tape.

Debbie Mumm's® Birdhouses for Every Season

CUTTING THE STRIPS AND PIECES

Read first paragraph of Cutting the Strips and Pieces on page 7.

		FIRST CUT		SECOND CUT	
		Number of Strips or Pieces	Dimensions	Number of Pieces	Dimensions
BIRDHOUSES		4	5½" x 3" (upper birdhouse)		
		4	4½" x 2" (birdhouse base)		
		4	4½" x 1" (birdhouse trim)		
		4	4½" x 2½" (middle birdhouse)		
		8	1" x 4½" (roof)		
		4	1½" squares (birdhouse holes)		
FABRIC A*		1	13½" x 24½"		
		8	3" squares		
		6	3" x 1½"		
		4	4½" x 2"		
		2	4½" x 2½"		
FABRIC B		2	1" x 42"	4	1" x 13½"
FABRIC C		1	3" x 42" (we used a "fussy cut" border)	2	3" x 13½"
FABRIC D		2	7½" x 14"		
BINDING		4	2¾" x 42"		

*We used directional fabric. Longer measurements are lengthwise.

MAKING THE BIRDHOUSE PANELS

You will be making two birdhouse panels to frame the appliquéd centerpiece of this project. Each panel includes two birdhouses made from a variety of scrap fabrics. Whenever possible, use the Assembly Line Method page on 110. Press in direction of arrows.

1. Refer to Quick Corner Triangle directions on page 110. Sew two 3" Fabric A squares to each 5½" x 3" upper birdhouse piece as shown. Press. Make four.

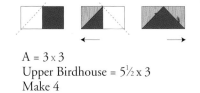

A = 3 x 3
Upper Birdhouse = 5½ x 3
Make 4

2. Sew three 3" x 1½" Fabric A pieces and two units from step 1 in order shown to make a horizontal row. Press. Make two.

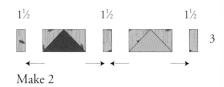

Make 2

3. Sew one 4½" x 1" birdhouse trim piece between one 4½" x 2" birdhouse base piece and one 4½" x 2½" middle birdhouse piece as shown. Press. Make four.

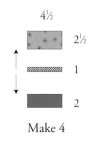

Make 4

4. Refer to layout on page 78 and color photo on page 81. Arrange and sew two 2" x 4½" Fabric A pieces, two units from step 3, and one 4½" x 2½" Fabric A piece in order shown to make a horizontal row. Press. Make two.

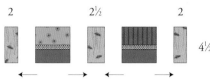

Make 2

5. Refer to layout and color photo. Sew rows from step 2 and step 4 together in pairs. Press. Make two panels. Panel will measure 13½" x 7".

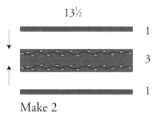

Make 2

6. Sew one 13½" x 3" Fabric C strip between two 13½" x 1" Fabric B strips. Press. Make two.

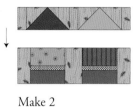

Make 2

7. Sew units from step 6 to bottom edge of each panel from step 5. Press.

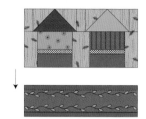

ASSEMBLY

1. Refer to layout on page 78 and color photo. Sew one birdhouse panel to each end of 13½"x 24½" Fabric A piece, taking care to position panels as shown. Press seams away from birdhouse panels.

2. Prepare points from Fabric D pieces. Fold each Fabric D piece in half along 14" side and press to mark center as shown. Align 45-degree mark on your ruler with center fold on each Fabric D piece. Trim away fabric triangle. Repeat on other side to create point.

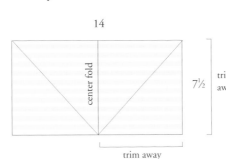

14

center fold

7½

trim away

trim away

3. Refer to layout and color photo. Sew one Fabric D triangle to each end of unit from step 1. Press seams away from points.

APPLIQUÉ

1. Refer to Quick-fuse Appliqué directions on page 111. Trace appliqué designs from page 83. Fuse four birdhouse holes and twelve leaves.

2. Finish edges using a machine blanket, satin, or small zigzag stitch or if preferred, hand appliqué referring to directions on page 110. Appliqué two 1" x 4½" roof strips on each birdhouse. Follow seam lines and square ends as shown.

LAYERING AND FINISHING

1. Cut backing fabric lengthwise into two equal pieces. Sew pieces together to make one 20" x 62" (approximate) backing piece. Arrange and baste backing, batting, and top together, referring to Layering the Quilt directions on page 111.

2. Hand or machine quilt as desired. Trim batting ¼" from raw edge of table runner.

3. Sew 2¾" x 42" binding strips together end to end to make one continuous 2¾" wide strip. From this strip, cut two 2¾" x 48" (approximate) binding strips. Sew these strips to long sides, extending strips at both ends as shown. Press binding away from table runner. Following angle of short sides, trim excess length of binding.

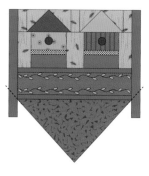

4. Cut four 2¾" x 12" binding strips from remaining 2¾"-wide strip. Sew one short binding strip to one side of each point. Press binding away from table runner. Trim excess length ¼" away from folded edge of side binding strip and even with raw edge on other end.

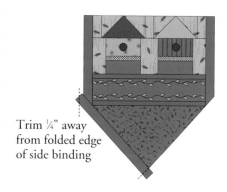

Trim ¼" away from folded edge of side binding

5. Sew remaining short binding strips to remaining sides. Press and trim ¼" away from folded edge of side binding strip and even with folded edge of binding strip on pointed end.

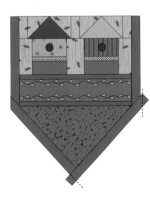

6. Press binding to back. Fold long sides first, then short sides with raw edge, then finally short sides with folded edge around to back. Press, pin in position, and hand stitch binding in place.

Birdhouse hole for
Falling Leaves Table Runner

Finished
Size ⅞"
Cut 4

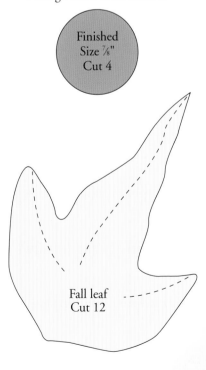

Fall leaf
Cut 12

Falling Leaves Placemats

These sweet 'n simple placemats partner perfectly with our table runner (see page 81). If you'd like, use the leaf pattern to trace, cut, and appliqué three or more leaves to each placemat center. Fabric requirements and cutting instructions are for a single placemat; make as many as you need for your harvest table. Read all instructions before beginning and use ¼"-wide seams throughout. Finished size will be 19" x 13".

FABRIC REQUIREMENTS

One Placemat:
Placemat Center - 19½" x 8½" piece
Border - Two 19½" x 2½" strips*
Binding - Two 2¾" x 20" strips
Backing - 24" x 17" piece

Lightweight Batting - 24" x 17" piece
* We chose a fussy cut for the border. If you choose to do the same, you may need to adjust the size of the placemat center.

ASSEMBLY AND FINISHING

1. Sew 19½" x 8½" placemat center piece between two 19½" x 2½" border strips. Press toward borders.

2. Position top and backing right sides together. Center both pieces on top of batting and pin all three layers together. Using ¼" seams, sew both 12½" edges.

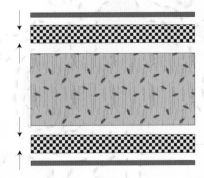

3. Trim stitched seams, turn placemats right side out, trim batting and backing ¼" from raw edge of placemat top.

4. Machine or hand quilt as desired.

5. Sew 2¾" x 20" binding strips to long edges, leaving ½" seam allowance extending beyond each end. Fold binding in half turning to back and press, tucking in raw edges to finish ends. Pin and hand stitch binding in place.

Winter

Outside the snow may be falling and the wintry wind blowing … but inside it's cozy and warm. Our heartier feathered friends find shelter in their snow-capped homes. Bright cardinals flit across the frosty ground on their winter rounds while cheery chickadees add their sweet songs to the snowy stillness.

You, too, can nestle snugly into wintertime. Just wrap yourself in a cozy quilt and enjoy working on these wonderful winter projects for your home. Outside the window—let it snow, let it snow!

Birdhouse Border Christmas Quilt

Holiday time *means a house brimming with loved ones, and an extra quilt is always welcome! No matter who is home for the holidays at your house, we're sure this clever quilt will be admired ... and happily used for years to come.*

Read all instructions *before beginning and use ¼" seams throughout.*

Birdhouse Border Christmas Quilt
Finished Quilt Size: 61" square
Photo: page 88

FABRIC REQUIREMENTS

Fabric A (Irish Chain) - ⅓ yard
Fabric B (Irish Chain) - ⅓ yard
Fabric C (Irish Chain Centers) ⅛ yard
Fabric D (Irish Chain) - ⅓ yard
Fabric E (Irish Chain) - ⅝ yard
Fabric F (Irish Chain and Star) 1 yard
Fabric G (Star Points) - ½ yard
Fabric H (Star Corners) - ¼ yard
Fabric I (Star Centers) - ½ yard
Fabric J (Corner Stars) - ⅛ yard
Fabric K (Corner Star Points) - ⅛ yard
Fabric L (Corner Star Centers) Scraps
Accent Border - ⅓ yard
Outside Border - ⅞ yard *

Binding - ⅔ yard
Backing - 4⅛ yard
Lightweight Batting - 69" x 69" piece

* If you select a border print as we did, you will need to increase the yardage, depending on the number of design repeats in the fabric.

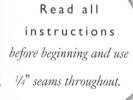

CUTTING THE STRIPS AND PIECES

Read first paragraph of Cutting the Strips and Pieces on page 7.

		FIRST CUT		SECOND CUT	
		Number of Strips or Pieces	Dimensions	Number of Pieces	Dimensions
	FABRIC A AND FABRIC B	4	2½" x 42" each color		
	FABRIC C	1	2½" x 42"		
	FABRIC D	4	2½" x 42"		
	FABRIC E	8	2½" x 42"		
	FABRIC F	4	2½" x 42"		
		8	2½" x 42"	48	2½" x 6½"
	FABRIC G	6	2½" x 42"	96	2½" squares
	FABRIC H	3	2½" x 42"	48	2½" squares
	FABRIC I	2	6½" x 42"	12	6½" squares
	FABRIC J	2	1½" x 42"	16	1½" x 2½"
				16	1½" squares
	FABRIC K	2	1½" x 42"	32	1½" squares
	FABRIC L	4	2½" squares		
	ACCENT BORDER	6	1½" x 42"		
	OUTSIDE BORDER	6	4½" x 42"		
	BINDING	8	2¾" x 42"		

MAKING THE BLOCKS

You will be making 13 Irish Chain blocks, 12 star blocks, and four small corner star blocks. Whenever possible, use the Assembly Line Method page 110. Press in direction of arrows.

Irish Chain Blocks

1. Sew 2½" x 42" strips together in the following order to make two identical strip sets: Fabric A, Fabric E, Fabric F, Fabric E, and Fabric A.* Press. Cut twenty-six 2½" segments.

*Sew each strip in opposite directions to prevent stretching.

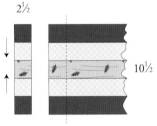

Make 2 strip sets
Cut 26

2. Repeat to sew 2½" x 42" strips together in the following order to make two identical strips sets: Fabric E, Fabric B, Fabric D, Fabric B, and Fabric E.* Press. Cut twenty-six 2½" segments.

*Sew each strip in opposite directions to prevent stretching.

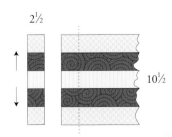

Make 2 strip sets
Cut 26

3. Sew 2½" x 42" strips together in the following order to make one strip set: Fabric F, Fabric D, Fabric C, Fabric D, and Fabric F.* Press. Cut thirteen 2½" segments.

*Sew each strip in opposite directions to prevent stretching.

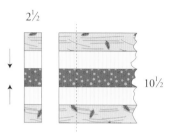

Make 1 strip set
Cut 13

4. Arrange two units from step 1, two units from step 2, and one unit from step 3 as shown. Sew rows together, carefully matching seams. Press. Make thirteen blocks.

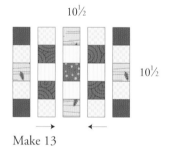

Make 13

Star Blocks

1. Refer to Quick Corner Triangle directions on page 110. Sew two 2½" Fabric G squares to each 2½" x 6½" Fabric F strip as shown. Press. Make forty-eight.

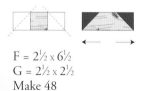

F = 2½ x 6½
G = 2½ x 2½
Make 48

2. Sew each 6½" Fabric I square between two units from step 1 as shown. Press. Make twelve.

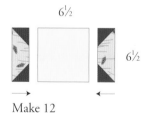

Make 12

3. Sew each remaining unit from step 1 between two 2½" Fabric H squares as shown. Press. Make twenty-four.

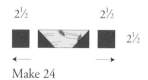

Make 24

4. Sew each unit from step 2 between two units from step 3. Press. Block measures 10½". Make twelve.

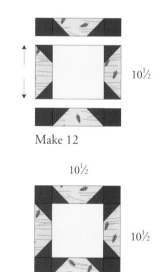

Make 12

88

Debbie Mumm's® Birdhouses for Every Season

ASSEMBLY

1. Refer to layout on page 86 and color photo. Alternate three Irish Chain blocks and two star blocks to make a horizontal row. Sew blocks together. Press seams toward Irish Chain blocks. Make three rows.

2. Refer to layout on page 86 and color photo. Alternate three star blocks and two Irish Chain blocks to make a horizontal row. Sew blocks together. Press seams toward Irish Chain Blocks. Make two rows.

3. Referring to the layout on page 86 and the color photo, lay out the rows from steps 1 and 2 as shown. Join the rows and press.

Corner Star Blocks

1. Refer to Quick Corner Triangle directions on page 110. Sew two 1½" Fabric K squares to each 1½" x 2½" Fabric J strip as shown. Press. Make sixteen.

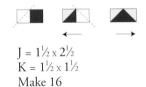

J = 1½ x 2½
K = 1½ x 1½
Make 16

2. Sew each 2½" Fabric L square between two units from step 1 as shown. Press. Make four.

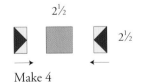

2½

2½

Make 4

3. Sew each remaining unit from step 1 between two 1½" Fabric J squares as shown. Press. Make eight.

1½   1½

1½

Make 8

4. Sew each unit from step 2 between two units from step 3. Press. Make four.

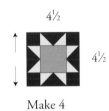

4½

4½

Make 4

BORDERS

1. Sew 1½" x 42" accent border strips end to end to make one continuous 1½"-wide strip. Measure quilt through center from side to side. Cut two 1½"-wide accent border strips to that measurement. Sew to top and bottom. Press seams toward border strips.

2. Measure quilt through center from top to bottom, including borders just added. Cut two 1½"-wide accent border strips to that measurement. Sew to sides. Press.

3. Sew 4½" x 42" outside border strips end to end to make one continuous 4½"-wide strip. Measure quilt through center from side to side, and from top to bottom. (This measurement should be the same.) Cut four 4½"-wide outside border strips to that measurement.

4. Sew two 4½"-wide outside border strips to top and bottom edges of quilt. Press.

5. Sew a corner star block to the ends of two remaining 4½"-wide outside border strips. Press seams toward border strips.

6. Sew borders from step 5 to sides of quilt. Press.

LAYERING AND FINISHING

1. Cut backing fabric crosswise into two equal pieces. Sew pieces together to make one 75" x 75" (approximate) backing piece. Arrange and baste backing, batting, and top together, referring to Layering the Quilt directions on page 111.

2. Machine or hand quilt as desired. On pages 90-91 we have provided quilting templates of bird houses which we used on the 6½" Fabric I squares.

3. Sew 2¾" x 42" binding strips in pairs. Refer to Binding the Quilt directions on page 111 and use the pieced binding strips to finish.

Quilting template
placement for blocks

QUILTING TEMPLATES

Use on the 6½" Fabric I squares, if
desired, for the Birdhouse Border
Christmas Quilt.

To transfer the quilting templates to
your quilt top:

1. Trace the template designs onto
6-inch squares of lightweight,
tear-away stabilizer.

2. Place the traced template over the
center block square and attach by using
a temporary fabric adhesive or pins.

3. Machine stitch on the traced lines,
starting in the center and continuing
toward the edges.

4. Carefully tear away the stabilizer.
(Waxed butcher paper may be used in
place of the stabilizer. Trace the design
onto the paper side of the butcher paper
and press the paper to the block with
a warm iron. Continue as above.)

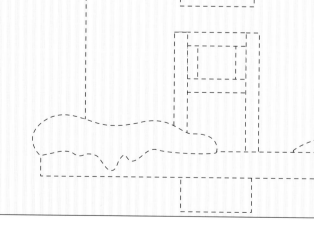

Winter ~ *Birdhouse Border Christmas Quilt*

Crimson Cardinals Table Quilt

Just as nature's *cardinals accent the winter landscape, our four bright red cardinals add a splash of vibrant color to this striking table topper.*

Instructions are for *hand appliqué techniques, but you can substitute quick-fuse methods if you prefer. Read all instructions before beginning and use ¼" seams throughout.*

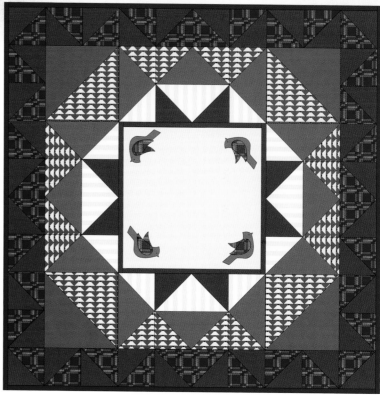

Crimson Cardinals Table Quilt
Finished Table Quilt Size: 41" square
Photo: page 95

FABRIC REQUIREMENTS

Fabric A (Center Block) - ½ yard
Fabric B (Dark Red Center and
   Sawtooth Border Triangles) - ⅞ yard
Fabric C (Tan Triangles) - ⅓ yard
Fabric D (Medium Red Triangles)
   ½ yard
Fabric E (Medium Green Triangles)
   ⅝ yard
Fabric F (Dark Green Corner
   Triangles) - ⅓ yard
Fabric G (Green Sawtooth Border
   Triangles) - ⅔ yard

Accent Border - ⅛ yard
Appliqués - Assorted red scraps
   for cardinal bodies and wings
Binding - ½ yard
Backing - 1¼ yards *
Lightweight Batting - 44" x 44" piece
Black Embroidery Floss

* Fabric must measure 45" wide.

CUTTING THE STRIPS AND PIECES

Read first paragraph of Cutting the Strips and Pieces on page 7.

		FIRST CUT		SECOND CUT	
		Number of Strips or Pieces	Dimensions	Number of Pieces	Dimensions
	FABRIC A	1	15½" square		
	FABRIC B	6	4½" x 42"	44	4½" squares
	FABRIC C	2	4½" x 42"	4 8	4½" x 8½" 4½" squares
	FABRIC D	3	4½" x 42"	12	4½" x 8½"
	FABRIC E	2 1	4½" x 42" 8½" x 42"	16 4	4½" squares 8½" squares
	FABRIC F	1	8½" x 42"	4	8½" squares
	FABRIC G	5	4½" x 42"	4 28	4½" x 8½" 4½" squares
	ACCENT BORDER	2	1" x 42"	2 2	1" x 15½" 1" x 16½"
	BINDING	5	2¾" x 42"		

MAKING THE CENTER PANEL

Whenever possible use the Assembly Line Method on page 110. Press in direction of arrows.

1. Sew 1" x 15½" accent border strips to opposite sides of 15½" Fabric A center block. Press seams toward accent border. Sew 1" x 16½" accent border strips to two remaining sides of block. Press.

2. Refer to Quick Corner Triangle directions on page 110. Sew two 4½" Fabric B squares to each 4½" x 8½" Fabric C piece as shown. Press. Make four.

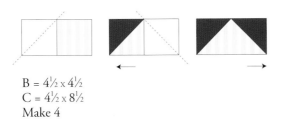

B = 4½ x 4½
C = 4½ x 8½
Make 4

3. Sew two 4½" Fabric E squares to one 4½" x 8½" Fabric D piece as shown. Press. Make four.

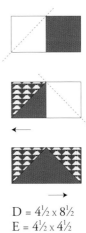

D = 4½ x 8½
E = 4½ x 4½
Make 4

4. Sew units from step 2 and step 3 together in pairs as shown. Press. Make four.

Make 4

5. Sew one 4½" Fabric C square and one 4½" Fabric E square to each remaining 4½" x 8½" Fabric D pieces as shown. Press. Make four of each variation.

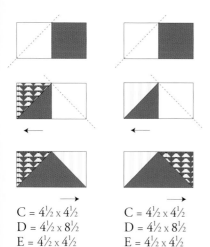

C = 4½ x 4½
D = 4½ x 8½
E = 4½ x 4½
Make 4

C = 4½ x 4½
D = 4½ x 8½
E = 4½ x 4½
Make 4

6. Sew each unit from step 4 between one of each unit from step 5 as shown. Press. Make four.

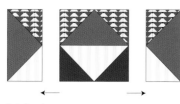

Make 4

7. Sew 8½" Fabric E and 8½" Fabric F squares together in pairs, referring to Quick Corner Triangle directions on page 110. Press. Make four.

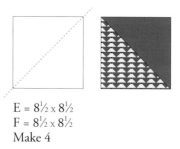

E = 8½ x 8½
F = 8½ x 8½
Make 4

8. Sew one unit from step 6 between two units from step 7 as shown. Press. Make two. Strip measures 32½" x 8½".

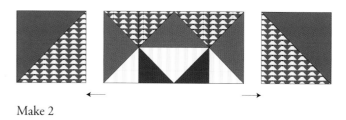

Make 2

9. Sew remaining units from step 6 to opposite sides of bordered center block. Press.

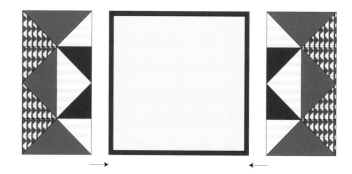

10. Sew units from step 8 to remaining sides. Press to outside.

Cardinal Appliqués

1. Trace appliqué designs from page 96. Make templates and use red scraps to trace four each of pieces 1 (under wing), 2 (body), 3 (top wing), and use gold or yellow fabric to trace four of piece 4 (beak). Cut out appliqués, adding ¼" seam allowance around each piece.

2. Referring to layout on page 92 and color photo, position appliqués in four corners of center block. Refer to Hand Appliqué directions on page 110 to stitch appliqués in place.

3. Referring to pattern on page 96 for placement, use two strands of black embroidery floss to make French knot eye for each cardinal. Add additional embroidered detail as desired. Refer to Embroidery Stitch Guide on page 110.

Sawtooth Border

1. Refer to Quick Corner Triangle directions on page 110. Sew two 4½" Fabric B squares to each 4½" x 8½" Fabric G piece as shown. Press. Make four.

B = 4½ x 4½
C = 4½ x 8½
Make 4

2. Sew remaining 4½" Fabric B and 4½" Fabric G squares together in pairs, referring to Quick Corner Triangle directions on page 110. Press. Make twenty-eight.

B = 4½ x 4½
G = 4½ x 4½
Make 28

3. Sew one unit from step 1 and six units from step 2 as shown. Press. Make four.

32½

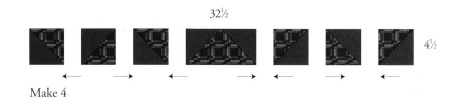

4½

Make 4

4. Referring to layout on page 92 and color photo on page 95, sew two units from step 3 to opposite sides of quilt. Press seams away from center panel.

5. Sew each remaining unit from step 3 between remaining units from step 2. Press.

40½

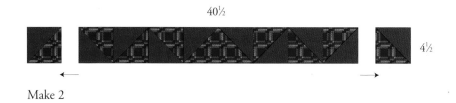

4½

Make 2

6. Sew units from step 5 to remaining sides of quilt. Press.

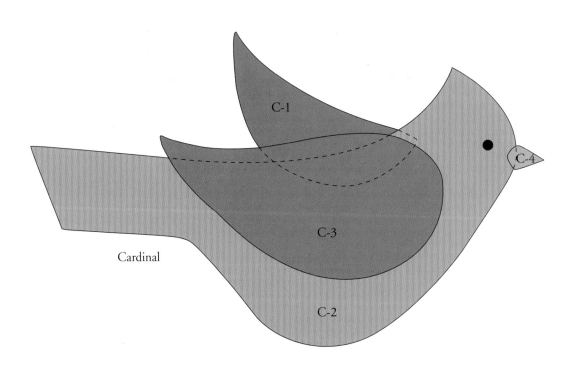

Cardinal

C-1

C-4

C-3

C-2

Birdfeeder

Here's a great wintertime treat for our feathered friends! Upside down feeders such as the nuthatch particularly enjoy it.

MATERIALS
Pinecones
Bird Seed
Bacon grease or other fat
Peanut Butter

1. Stir equal portions of peanut butter, bacon grease or other discarded fat, and bird seed.

2. Tie a sturdy string to fir cones or pinecones and roll in mixture.

3. Hang from a tree limb.

LAYERING AND FINISHING

1. Arrange and baste backing, batting, and top together, referring to Layering the Quilt directions on page 111.

2. Machine or hand quilt as desired.

3. Using the five 2¾" x 42" binding strips, refer to Binding the Quilt directions on page 111 to finish.

Winter Birds Mantel Cover

Winter Birds Mantel Cover
Finished Panel Size: 8" x 18"
Photo: page 100

A fragrant, crackling fire *becomes even more inviting when your mantel is dressed in our charming four-panel mantel topper. We've hand appliquéd the birds, or you can quick-fuse them as we have the snowflakes and flowers.*

It's up to you! *We've also included tips for easily hanging this wonderful wintertime creation. Read all instructions before beginning and use ¼" seams throughout.*

FABRIC REQUIREMENTS

Background - 1 yard *

Appliqués - Assorted scraps for birds, snowflakes, and poinsettias

Binding - ½ yard

Embroidery Floss

Lightweight Batting - Four 10" x 20" pieces (optional)

* May substitute ¼ yard each of four different green fabrics.

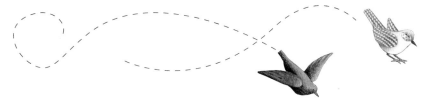

CUTTING THE STRIPS AND PIECES

Read first paragraph of Cutting the Strips and Pieces on page 7.

		FIRST CUT		SECOND CUT	
		Number of Strips or Pieces	Dimensions	Number of Pieces	Dimensions
	BACK-GROUND	4	8" x 36"		
	BINDING	5	2¾" x 42"	8	2¾" x 15"
				8	2¾" x 10"

PREPARING BACKGROUND PANELS

1. Fold each 8" x 36" background panel in half lengthwise and press to mark center as shown. Align 45-degree mark on your ruler with center fold on background fabric. Trim away fabric triangle on one short end of background fabric. Repeat on other end to create points.

2. Repeat step 1 on other 8" ends of each background panel.

APPLIQUE AND EMBROIDERY

1. Refer to Quick-Fuse Appliqué directions on page 110. Trace appliqué designs for pieces 1-3 on page 101. Prepare two of piece 1 (snowflake), and four each of pieces 2 and 3 (poinsettia).

2. Refer to layout on page 98 and color photo on page 100. Center and fuse one snowflake appliqué 2½" from one point on two background panels.

3. Center, stack, and fuse two of each poinsettia appliqués 2½" from one point on each remaining background panel.

4. Trace appliqué designs for cardinal, wren, junco, and goldfinch from pages 96, 101, and 108. Make templates and use scraps to trace one of each pattern piece. Cut out appliqués, add ¼" seam allowance around each piece if using hand appliqué. If using Quick-fuse method reverse bird appliqué patterns.

5. Referring to pattern layout on page 98, and color photo on page 100, position one bird on each panel.

6. Machine stitch or refer to Hand Appliqué on page 110. Stitch appliqués in place. Begin with Piece 1 and work numerically as indicated on patterns.

7. Use two strands of yellow embroidery floss to make french knot centers for each poinsettia. Use two strands of black embroidery floss to make french knot eye for each bird. Add additional embroidered detail as desired. Refer to Embroidery Stitch Guide on page 110.

ASSEMBLY AND FINISHING

1. Fold background fabric in half wrong sides together, matching points as shown. Press the fold. Place a lightweight batting in center flush with fold. Hand or pin baste through all layers, and baste around cut edges.

2. Hand or machine quilt as desired.

3. Trim batting to ¼" from raw edges of mantel covers.

4. Sew 2¾" x 15" binding strips to long sides of each panel. Extend strip ¼" past folded edge, and leave excess extending beyond bottom edge as shown. Press binding away from panel. Following angle of short sides, trim excess length of binding on bottom edge only.

5. Sew one 2¾" x 10" binding strip to one side of each point. Press binding away from panel. Trim excess length ¼" away from folded edge of side binding strip and even with raw edge on other end. Press to outside edges.

Trim ¼" away
from folded edge
of side binding

6. Sew remaining short binding strips to remaining side of each point. Press and trim ¼" away from folded edge of side binding strip and even with folded edge of binding strip on pointed end.

7. Press binding to outside. Fold long sides first, then short sides with raw edge, and finally short sides with folded edge around to back. Pin and hand stitch binding in place.

Make a display

To display your mantel covers, place four inches on the mantle and allow the rest to hang. You may set your decorations on top to hold the covers in place, secure with tape; or attach velcro flush with and 4" from the folded edge, fasten the velcro and insert a narrow rod or slat to secure.

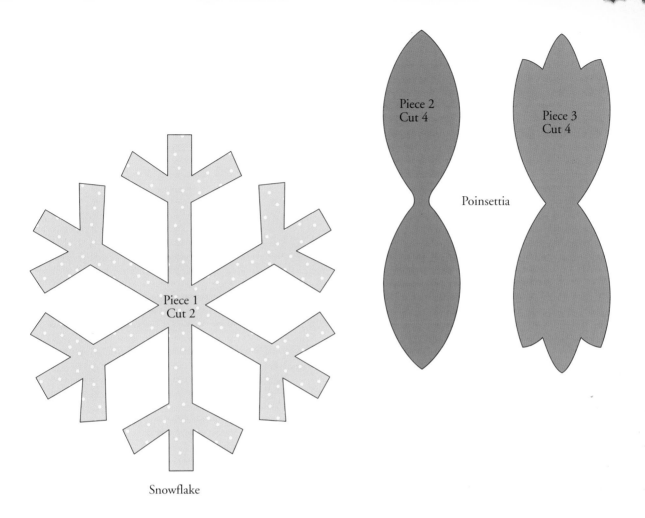

Piece 1
Cut 2

Snowflake

Piece 2
Cut 4

Poinsettia

Piece 3
Cut 4

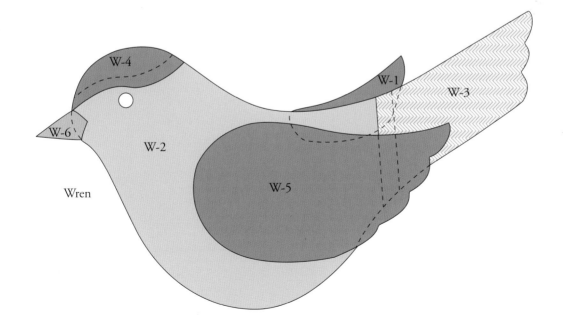

W-4

W-1

W-3

W-6

W-2

W-5

Wren

Birdhouse Banner

Birdhouse Banner
Finished Quilt Size: 21" x 23½"
Photos: pages 104 and 105

Here's a clever *idea ... a bright and beautiful birdhouse banner with easy-to-change trims to welcome each season. There are three methods for creating the various seasonal adornments and three ways to attach them.*

Choose the option *you like best! Read all instructions before beginning and use ¼" seams throughout.*

FABRIC REQUIREMENTS

Fabric A (Roof and Chimney Top)
   ⅛ yard
Fabric B (Background) - ¼ yard
Fabric C (Branches) - Scraps
Fabric D (House) - ⅙ yard
Fabric E (Shutters) - Scraps
Fabric F (Door Trim) - Scraps
Fabric G (Door) - Scrap
Fabric H (House Trim) - Scraps
Fabric I (House Base and Chimney)
   ⅛ yard
Fabric J (Birdhouse Stand and Post)
   ⅛ yard
Birdhouse Hole Appliqué - Scrap
Birds and Other Seasonal
   Trims - Assorted Scraps
Accent Border - ⅛ yard

Outside Border - ¼ yard
Binding - ⅓ yard
Backing - ⅞ yard
Lightweight Batting - 23" x 26" piece
Embroidery Floss
Scraps of heavy-duty fusible web
Scraps of lightweight batting
   (optional) *
Assorted small buttons (optional) *
Small hooks *

* Whether you need these notions will
   be determined by the methods you
   choose to construct and attach the
   birds and other seasonal trims.
   See pages 106 and 107.

CUTTING THE STRIPS AND PIECES

Read first paragraph of Cutting the Strips and Pieces on page 7.

		FIRST CUT		SECOND CUT	
		Number of Strips or Pieces	Dimensions	Number of Pieces	Dimensions
■	FABRIC A	2	1" x 42"	1 1 1 1 1 1 1	8½" x 1" 9" x 1" 9½" x 1" 10" x 1" 10½" x 1" 11" x 1" 3" x 1"
▨	FABRIC B	1	1" x 42"	14 2 2 2 2	1" squares 1¾" x 1" 1½" x 1" 1¼" x 1" ¾" x 1"
		2 2 2 2 1	2¾" x 3½" 3" x 8½" 7¼" x 2" 7" x 2" 15½" x 2½"		
■	FABRIC C	1	1¼" x 20"		Bias cut recommended
▨	FABRIC D	2 1 2 2	3¼" x 2¾" 2½" x 2¾" 3¾" x 4¼" 9½" x 1"		
■	FABRIC E	2	1¼" x 2¾"		
■	FABRIC F	1 2	2½" x ¾" ¾" x 4¼"		
▨	FABRIC G	1	2½" x 4"		
■	FABRIC H	2	1" x 7½"		
▨	FABRIC I	1 1	10½" x 1½" 2½" x 2"		
■	FABRIC J	1 1	2" square 15½" x 2"		
■	ACCENT BORDER	2	1" x 42"	2 2	1" x 15½" 1" x 19"
■	OUTSIDE BORDER	2	2½" x 42"	2 2	2½" x 16½" 2½" x 23"
	BACKING	1	24" x 27"		
■	BINDING	3	2¾" x 42"		

MAKING THE BIRDHOUSE BLOCK

You will be making one birdhouse block. Whenever possible, use the Assembly Line Method on page 110 for each step. Press in direction of arrows.

> **Helpful Hint**
>
> *Since this block involves many similarly sized (but not identical) pieces, you may wish to label each piece with masking tape marked with its measurements.*

1. Refer to Quick Corner Triangle directions on page 110. Sew two 1" Fabric B squares to 8½" x 1" Fabric A strip, and label pieced strip as shown. Press. Repeat to sew two 1" Fabric B squares to 9" x 1" Fabric A strip, 9½" x 1" Fabric A strip, 10" x 1" Fabric A strip, 10½"x 1" Fabric A strip, and 11" x 1" Fabric A strip. Label and press.

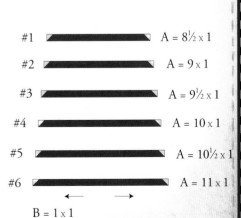

#1   A = 8½ x 1

#2   A = 9 x 1

#3   A = 9½ x 1

#4   A = 10 x 1

#5   A = 10½ x 1

#6   A = 11 x 1

B = 1 x 1

2. Using strips pieced in step 1, sew strip #1 between two 1¾" x 1" Fabric B pieces as shown. Press. Repeat to sew strip #2 between two 1½" x 1" Fabric B pieces, strip #3 between two 1¼" x 1" Fabric B pieces, strip #4 between two 1" Fabric B squares, and strip # 5 between two ¾" x 1" Fabric B pieces. Press.

3. Arrange and sew roof strips 1-5 and #6 from step 1 in order shown to make a vertical row. Press. Unit will measure 11" x 3½".

4. Sew unit from step 3 between two 2¾" x 3½" Fabric B pieces as shown. Press.

5. Arrange and sew two 3¼" x 2¾" Fabric D pieces, two 1¼" x 2¾" Fabric E pieces, and one 2½" x 2¾" Fabric D piece in order shown to make a horizontal row. Press.

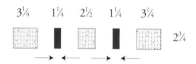

6. Sew 2½" x ¾" Fabric F piece to 2½" x 4" Fabric G piece as shown. Press.

7. Sew unit from step 6 between two ¾" x 4¼" Fabric F pieces. Press.

8. Sew unit from step 7 between two 3¾" x 4¼" Fabric D pieces. Press.

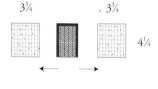

9. Arrange and sew one 9½" x 1" Fabric D strip, unit from step 5, remaining 9½" x 1" Fabric D strip, and unit from step 8 in order shown to make a vertical row. Press.

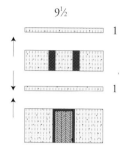

10. Sew unit from step 9 between two 1" x 7½" Fabric H strips. Press.

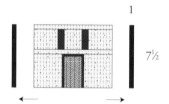

Summer Birdhouse Banner with Peaches and Finches

104

11. Sew 10½" x 1½" Fabric I strip to unit from step 10 as shown. Press.

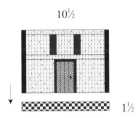

10½

1½

12. Sew unit from step 11 between two 3" x 8½" Fabric B pieces. Press.

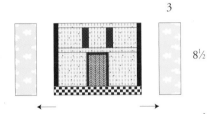

3

8½

13. Sew 2" Fabric J square between two 7¼" x 2" Fabric B pieces. Press.

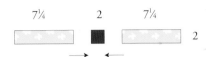

7¼   2   7¼   2

14. Sew 15½" x 2" Fabric J strip to unit from step 13 as shown. Press.

15½

2

15. Sew 2½" x 2" Fabric I piece between two 7" x 2" Fabric B pieces. Press.

7   2½   7   2

16. Arrange and sew 15½" x 2½" Fabric B strip, unit from step 15, unit from step 4, unit from step 12, and unit from step 14 in order shown to make a vertical row. Press.

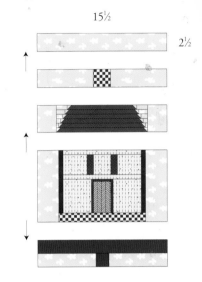

15½   2½

Spring Birdhouse Banner with Dogwood and Bluebirds

Autumn Birdhouse Banner with Maples and Juncos

Winter Birdhouse Banner with Holly and Cardinals

17. Trace birdhouse hole appliqué design from page 109. Make template and use scrap to cut one birdhouse hole, adding ¼" seam allowance.

18. Refer to Hand Appliqué directions on page 110. Referring to layout on page 102 and color photo on page 105, appliqué 3" x 1" chimney top over chimney, and birdhouse hole between shutters on house front. Position and appliqué branches to block background, trimming 1¼" x 20" bias strip into segments as needed.

BORDERS

1. Sew 1" x 15½" accent border strips to top and bottom of block. Press toward border strips. Repeat to sew 1" x 19" accent border strips to sides. Press.

2. Sew 2½" x 16½" outside border strips to top and bottom. Press toward outside border strips. Repeat to sew 2½" x 23" outside border strips to sides. Press.

LAYERING AND FINISHING

1. Arrange and baste backing, batting, and top together referring to Layering the Quilt directions on page 111.

2. Hand or machine quilt as desired.

3. Sew 2¾" x 42" binding strips end to end to make one continuous 2¾"-wide binding strip. Refer to Binding the Quilt directions on page 111 to finish.

Tip

Details such as bird wings may be assembled (layered, traced, stitched, and cut) separately, then tacked to main piece.

SEASONAL TRIMS

We used three methods for making birds and other seasonal trims for the banner. You may use one method, or any combination, to create the various trims.

Method 1:

1. We used this method for the dogwood leaf, peach leaf, and fall leaf. Refer to patterns for birds and seasonal trims on pages 96, 108, and 109. Make templates and trace required number of pieces onto heavy-duty fusible web. Follow manufacturer's directions to iron fusible web to wrong side of appropriately colored scraps. Cut designs along traced lines.

2. Cut a 6" square (approximate) of fabric to match main fabric in bird or seasonal trim. Fuse pieces from step 1 to wrong side of appropriate 6" square, layering them in numerical order as indicated on pattern.

3. Cut out bird or seasonal trim along outside edge of finished shape.

4. Refer to pattern, and use three strands of embroidery floss to make birds' eyes, and/or add other details. Refer to Embroidery Stitch Guide on page 110.

Method 2:

1. We used this method for peaches and dogwood blossoms. Refer to patterns for birds and seasonal trims on pages 96, 108 and 109. Trace required number of complete bird or seasonal trim outlines onto dull side of freezer paper.

2. Cut two matching 6" squares (approximate) of main bird or seasonal trim fabric. Layer as for quilting (one 6" square right side down, batting, one 6" square right side up).

3. Use a warm iron to press freezer paper shiny side down on top side of appropriate fabric "sandwich." Stitch directly on traced line, using a small stitch.

4. Remove freezer paper. Trim close to stitching with straight edge or pinking shears.

5. Follow manufacturer's directions and use fusible web to trace and beaks, breasts, wings, and tails to bird bodies, and details to seasonal trims.

6. Refer to pattern, and use three strands of embroidery floss to make birds' eyes, and/or add other details. Refer to Embroidery Stitch Guide on page 110.

Tips

Buttons may be substituted for dogwood centers and holly berries.

In some cases, fabrics may be stitched together before tracing and cutting; such as for goldfinch body and tail, etc.

Method 3:

1. We used this method for the birds and holly leaves. Refer to patterns for birds and seasonal trims on pages 96, 108 and 109. Trace one complete bird or seasonal trim outline onto template material.

2. Cut two matching 6" squares (approximate) of main bird or seasonal trim fabric. Place squares right sides together, and layer over 6" square of thin batting.

3. Place full outline template on wrong side of top fabric and trace. Stitch on traced lines, using a small stitch.

4. Trim close to stitching. Cut a small slit in top fabric only, and turn right side out.

5. Follow manufacturer's directions and use fusible web to trace and fuse beaks, breasts, wings, and tails to bird bodies, and details to seasonal trims.

6. Refer to pattern, and use three strands of embroidery floss to make birds' eyes, and/or add other details. Refer to Embroidery Stitch Guide on page 110.

ATTACHING TRIMS

You may use one of three methods to attach birds and trims to banner. Refer to layout on page 102, and color photos on page 104 and 105 for placement guidance as needed.

Method 1:

Sew buttons to banner as indicated. Make buttonholes in trims to attach.

Method 2:

Sew buttons to banner as indicated. Sew thread loop to back of each trim. Hook loops over buttons to attach.

Method 3:

Sew ⅜" thread loops to branches and background as desired. Attach hook to back of each trim. Hook trim to thread loop on banner.

● Indicates button placement

◆ Indicates loop placement

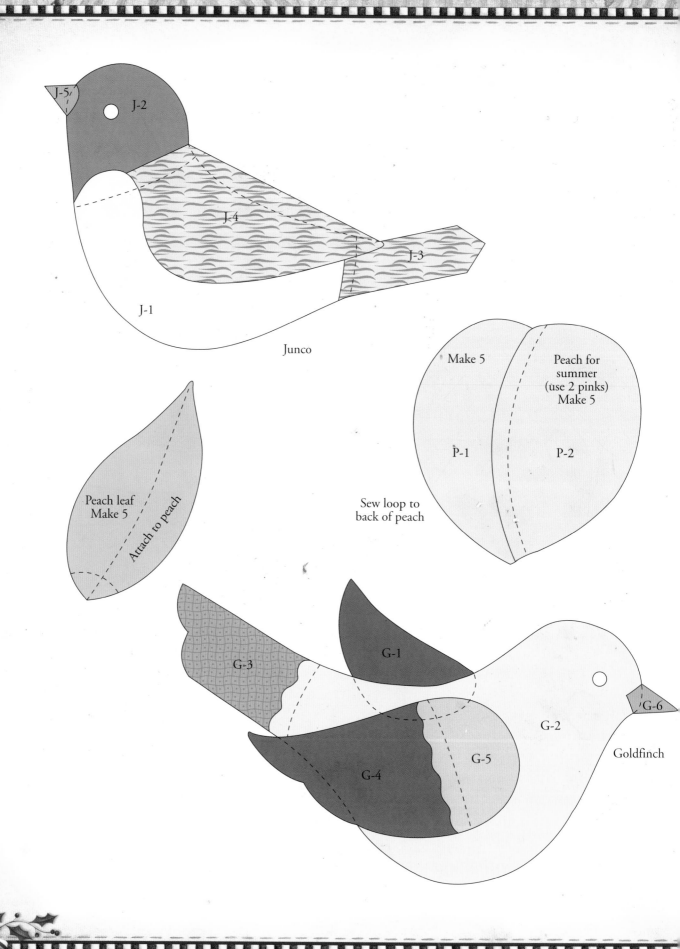

J-5

J-2

J-4

J-3

J-1

Junco

Make 5

Peach for summer (use 2 pinks) Make 5

P-1

P-2

Peach leaf Make 5

Attach to peach

Sew loop to back of peach

G-3

G-1

G-6

G-2

G-5

G-4

Goldfinch

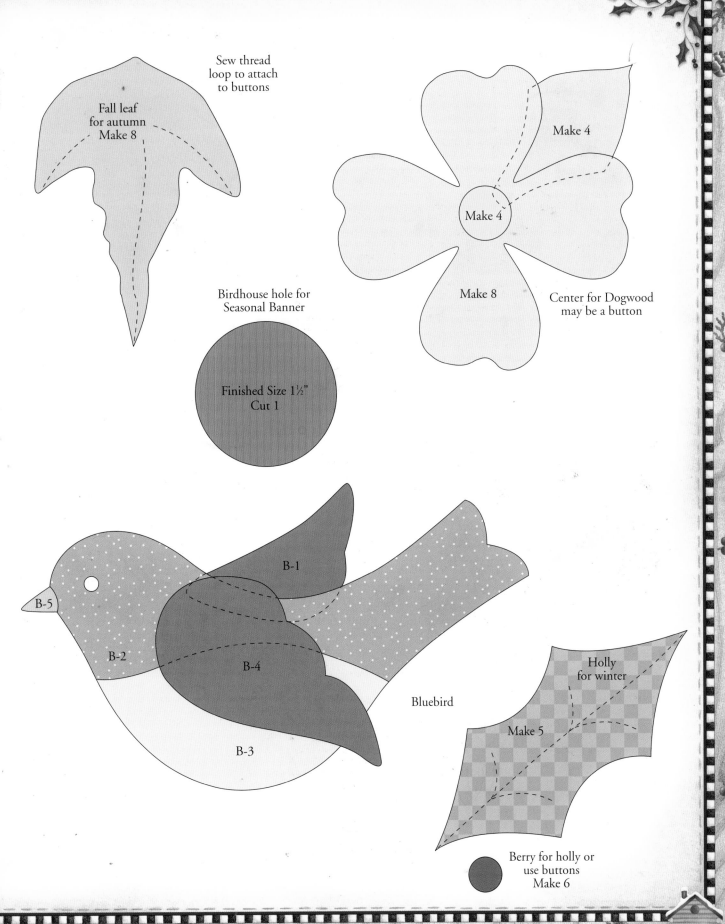

Sew thread
loop to attach
to buttons

Fall leaf
for autumn
Make 8

Make 4

Make 4

Make 8

Birdhouse hole for
Seasonal Banner

Finished Size 1½"
Cut 1

Center for Dogwood
may be a button

B-1

B-5

B-2

B-4

B-3

Bluebird

Holly
for winter

Make 5

Berry for holly or
use buttons
Make 6

ASSEMBLY LINE METHOD

Whenever possible, use the assembly line method. Position pieces right sides together and line up next to sewing machine. Stitch first unit together, then continue sewing others without breaking threads. When all units are sewn, clip threads to separate. Press in direction of arrows.

HAND APPLIQUÉ

Hand appliqué is easy when you start out with the right supplies. Cotton machine embroidery thread is easy to work with. Pick a color that matches the appliqué fabric as closely as possible. Use a long, thin needle, like a sharp, for stitching and slender appliqué or silk pins for holding shapes in place.

I. Make a plastic template for every shape in the appliqué design. Use a dotted line to show where pieces overlap.

2. Place template on right side of appliqué fabric. Trace around template.

3. Cut out shapes ¼" beyond traced line.

4. Position shapes on background fabric. For pieces that overlap, follow numbers on patterns. Pieces with lower numbers go underneath; pieces with higher numbers are layered on top. Pin shapes in place.

5. Stitch shapes in order following pattern numbers. Where shapes overlap, do not turn under and stitch edges of bottom pieces. Turn and stitch the edges of the piece on top.

6. Use the traced line as your turn-under guide. Entering from the wrong side of the appliqué shape, bring the needle up on the traced line. Using the tip of the needle, turn under the fabric along the traced line.

Using a blind stitch, stitch along the folded edge to join the appliqué shape to the background fabric. Turn under and stitch about ¼" at a time.

7. Clip curves and V-shapes to help the fabric turn under smoothly. Clip to within a couple threads of the traced line.

8. After stitching the entire block, place it face down on top of a thick towel and press.

QUICK CORNER TRIANGLES

Quick corner triangles are formed by simply sewing fabric squares to other squares and rectangles. The directions and diagrams with each project show you what size pieces to use and where to place square on corresponding piece. Follow steps 1–3 below to make corner triangle units.

I. With pencil and ruler, draw diagonal line on wrong side of fabric square that will form the triangle. See Diagram A. This will be your sewing line.

A.

sewing line

2. With right sides together, place square on corresponding piece. Matching raw edges, pin in place and sew ON drawn line. Trim off excess fabric leaving ¼" seam allowance as shown in Diagram B.

B.
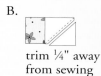
trim ¼" away from sewing

3. Press seam in direction of arrow as shown in step-by-step project diagram. Measure completed corner triangle unit to ensure greatest accuracy.

C.

finished corner triangle unit

EMBROIDERY STITCH GUIDE

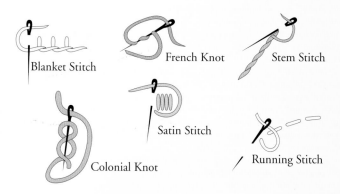

Blanket Stitch

French Knot

Stem Stitch

Colonial Knot

Satin Stitch

Running Stitch

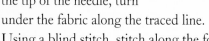

110

General Directions

LAYERING THE QUILT

1. Cut backing and batting 4" to 8" larger than quilt top.

2. Lay pressed backing on bottom (right side down), batting in middle, and pressed quilt top (right side up) on top. Make sure everything is centered and that backing and batting are flat. Backing and batting will extend beyond quilt top.

3. Begin basting in center and work toward outside edges. Baste vertically and horizontally, forming a 3" – 4" grid. Baste or pin completely around edge of quilt top. Quilt as desired.

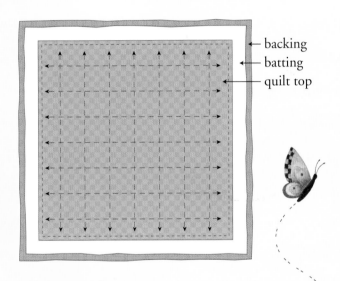

- backing
- batting
- quilt top

BINDING THE QUILT

1. Trim batting and backing to ¼" from raw edge of quilt top.

2. Fold and press binding strips in half lengthwise with wrong sides together.

3. With raw edges even, lay binding strips on top and bottom edges of quilt top. Sew through all layers, ¼" from quilt edge. Press binding away from quilt top. Trim excess length of binding.

4. Sew remaining two binding strips to quilt sides. Press and trim excess length.

5. Folding top and bottom first, fold binding around to back then repeat with sides. Press and pin in position. Hand stitch binding in place.

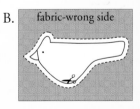

← fold top and bottom binding in first

QUICK-FUSE APPLIQUÉ

Quick-fuse appliqué is a method of adhering appliqué pieces to a background with fusible web. For quick and easy results, simply quick-fuse appliqué pieces in place. Use sewable, lightweight fusible web for the projects in this book unless indicated otherwise. Finishing raw edges with stitching is desirable. Laundering is not recommended unless edges are finished.

1. With paper side up, lay fusible web over appliqué design. Leaving ½" space between pieces, trace all elements of design. Cut around traced pieces, approximately ¼" outside traced line. See Diagram A.

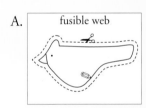

A. fusible web

2. With paper side up, position and iron fusible web to wrong side of selected fabrics. Follow manufacturer's directions for iron temperature and fusing time. Cut out each piece on traced line. See Diagram B.

B. fabric-wrong side

3. Remove paper backing from pieces. A thin film will remain on wrong side. Position and fuse all pieces of one appliqué design at a time onto background, referring to color photos for placement.

Discover More From Debbie Mumm®

Here's a sampling of some of the many other quilting and home décor books by Debbie Mumm. These books and specially designed patterns are available at your local quilt shop or by calling (888) 819-2923, or shop on-line at **www.debbiemumm.com**. When you order a Debbie Mumm® book, you'll receive a complimentary catalog filled with Debbie's most recent books, patterns, and selected gifts.
A $3 value, yours with a purchase.

Debbie Mumm's®
12 Days of Christmas
140-page, soft cover

Debbie Mumm's®
Country Settings
112-page, soft cover

Debbie Mumm's®
Project Kids™
64-page, soft cover

Woodland Christmas
80-page, soft cover

Cottage In Bloom
40-page, soft cover

Friendship Quilt Collection
36-page, soft cover

Winter Birds
pattern

Guardian Angel
pattern

Peace Quilt
pattern

1116 E. Westview Ct.,
Spokane, WA 99218
(509) 466-3572

Toll Free (888) 819-2923
Fax (509) 466-6919

www.debbiemumm.com

CREDITS

Designs by Debbie Mumm®
Special thanks to my creative teams:

EDITORIAL/PROJECT DESIGN

Carolyn Ogden: Managing Editor

Laura Reinstatler: Editor

Darra Williamson: Writer

Pam Mostek: Writer

Georgie Gerl: Quilt and Craft Designer

Carolyn Lowe: Quilt and Craft Designer

Susan Nelsen: Quilt and Craft Designer

Jackie Saling: Craft Designer

Candy Huddleston: Seamstress

Nancy Kirkland: Seamstress

Wanda Jeffries: Machine Quilter

Nona King: Machine Quilter

Pam Clarke: Machine Quilter

BOOK DESIGN & PRODUCTION

Mya Brooks: Production Director

Tom Harlow: Graphics Manager

Sherry Hassel: Sr. Graphic Designer

Heather Hughes: Graphic Designer

Quad/Photo

ART TEAM

Lou McKee, Sr. Artist

Kathy Arbuckle

Sandy Ayars

Heather Butler

Gil-Jin Foster

Kathy Riedinger

MARKETING/PR

Barbara Reinhardt: Director of Sales and Marketing

©2001 Mumm's The Word®, Inc.
Printed in Hong Kong